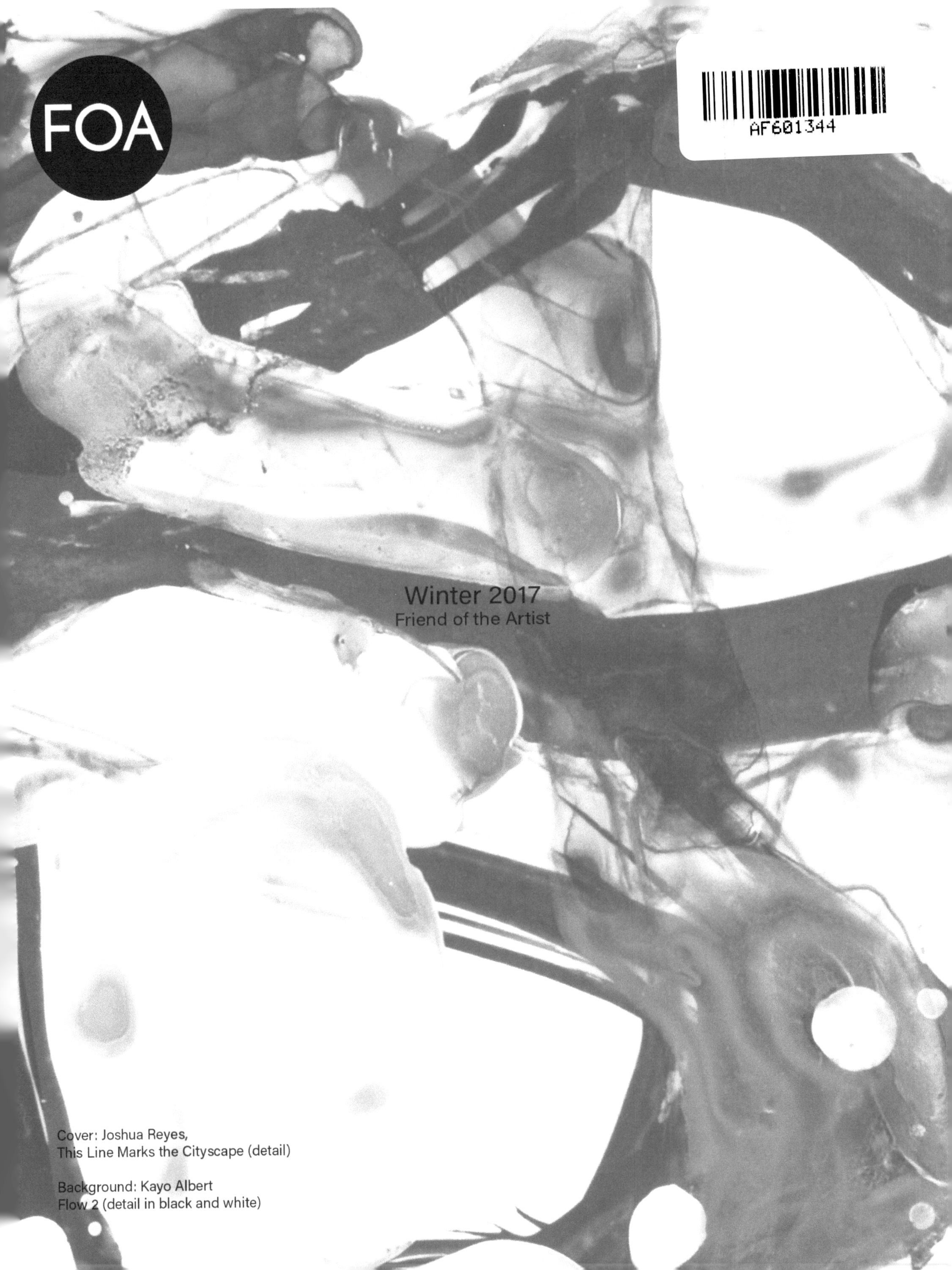

Cover: Joshua Reyes,
This Line Marks the Cityscape (detail)

Background: Kayo Albert
Flow 2 (detail in black and white)

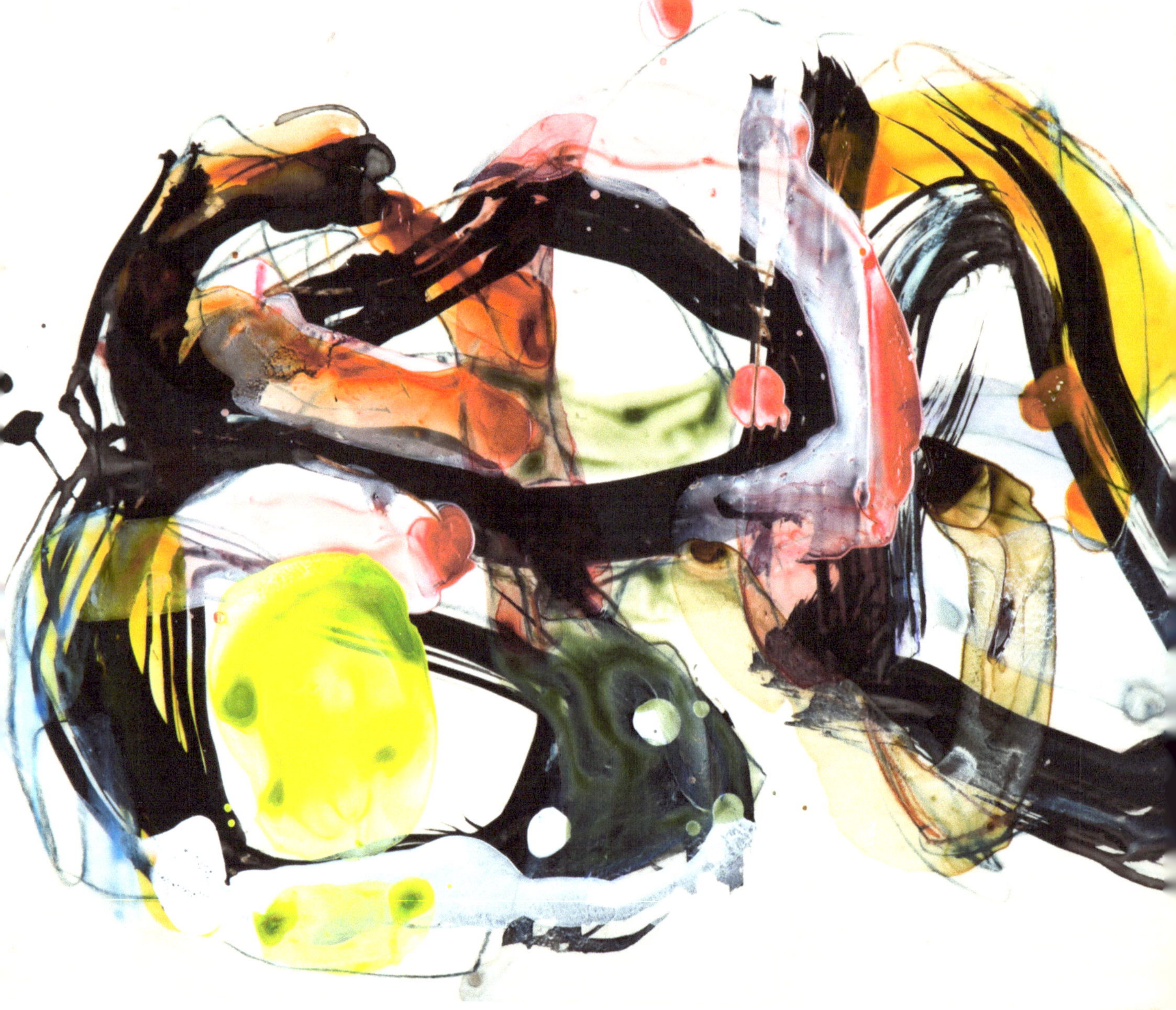

Kayo Albert, Flow 2

Friend of the Artist (FOA)
friendoftheartist.com
contact@friendoftheartist.com

Produced and printed in United States of America.

Design Help by Dannie Liebergot
Editing by Sarah Bishop

ISBN: 9780692844656

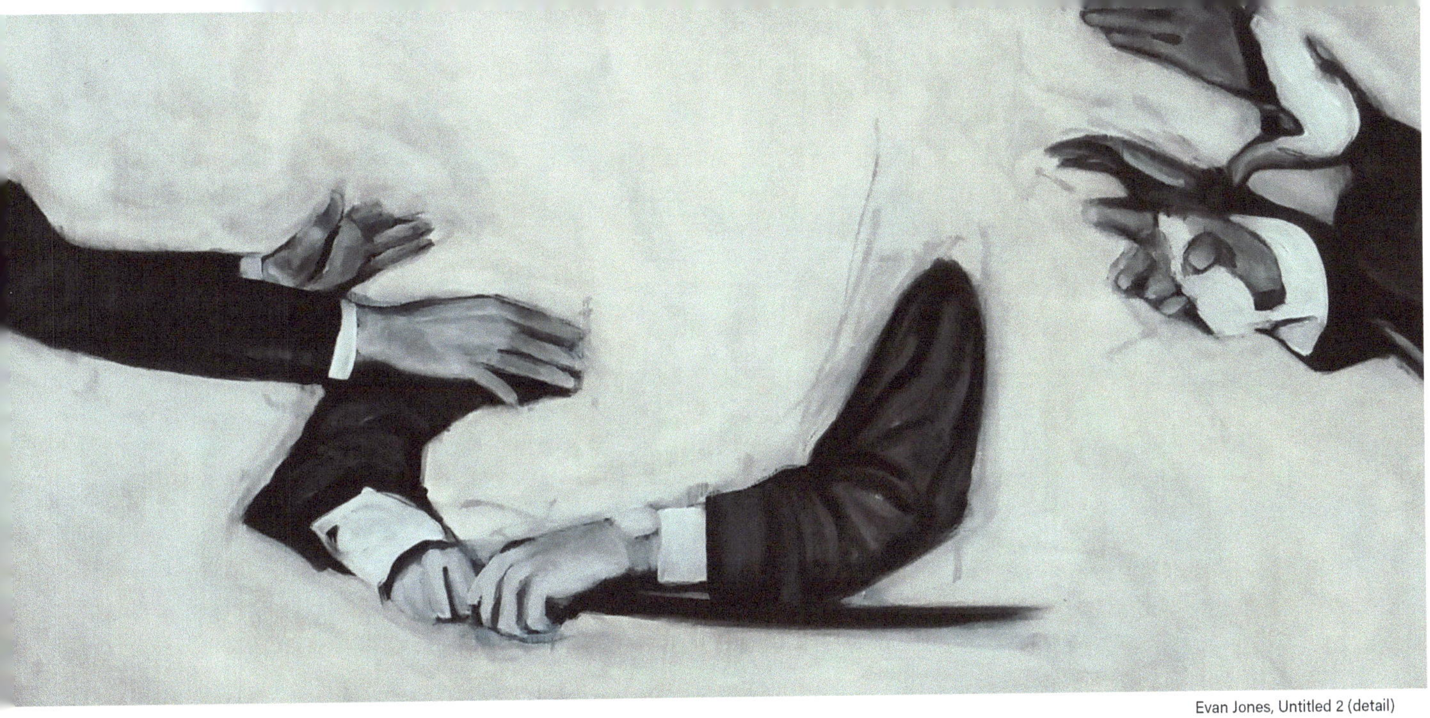

Evan Jones, Untitled 2 (detail)

Contents

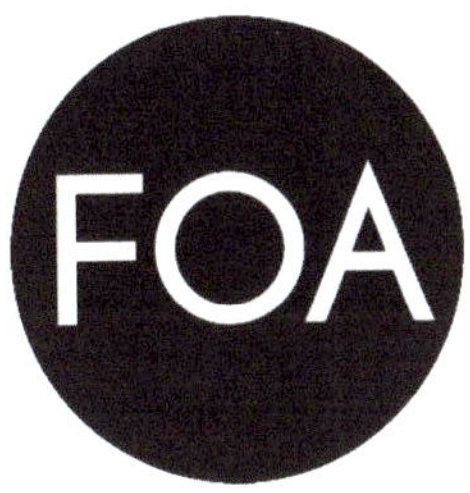

About FOA

Holding his painting stretched out on his back like a crucifix, Paul Cezanne, one of the most influential painters from the 20th century, carried his works to the prestigious French Salon. Though his submissions to the French Salon were never accepted, he is considered the father of Modern art. Through difficult times and discouragement, Cezanne was support by his friends Emile Zola and Camille Pissarro. Zola and Pissaro supported him through their words, resources, and finances which were a vital part of Cezanne's success.

This is precisely the role of FOA: to be a friend of the artist by supporting and showcasing the work of dedicated emerging artists.

Friend of the Artist is a quarterly print publication and online art space that showcases the work of artists from around the world. Artists represented in each publication are selected by a juror and must show immense facility and intellectual understanding of art history and the medium they use. FOA recognizes that existing as an artist outside an academic context is difficult. We function as a support structure between artists work, the art world, and an art audience. In addition, FOA also awards the top three artists of each publication with an in depth interview and awards one artist a cash prize.

Notes from the Editors

Ty Bishop

Artists are some the most interesting people you will ever talk to. They are dedicated individuals who spend their time, thoughts, and money devoted to one thing: art. Often the fruit they see in return for the many hours they put in their work is small. Despite set backs, they continue to make work and develop thier ideas whether it be aesthetic or conceptual. It seems mysterious to most people why anyone would actually choose to do this, and is highly irrational to a "bottom line" mindset. It was a privilege to sit down with these artists and diagloge with them about their work and reasons why they make it. I left the conversations with more questions than when I began.

Justin Archer

When we first began talking about Friend of the Artist, Ty and I were excited to create a platform to help other artists through funding and exposure. One of the things I didn't fully account for was how many artists we would have the opportunity to engage with. Through the jurying process, the interviewing, and all of the other attributes that make FOA a friend to artists, I have found so much joy. The unique opportunity we have had to talk with artists about their art making process, what drives them to create, and what their interested in communicating has by far been the most exciting part of FOA for me. As we continue learning more about other visual artists, we are continuing to create a larger web, connecting people from all across the United States and beyond. I am immensely thankful for all those who have participated in making FOA what it is.

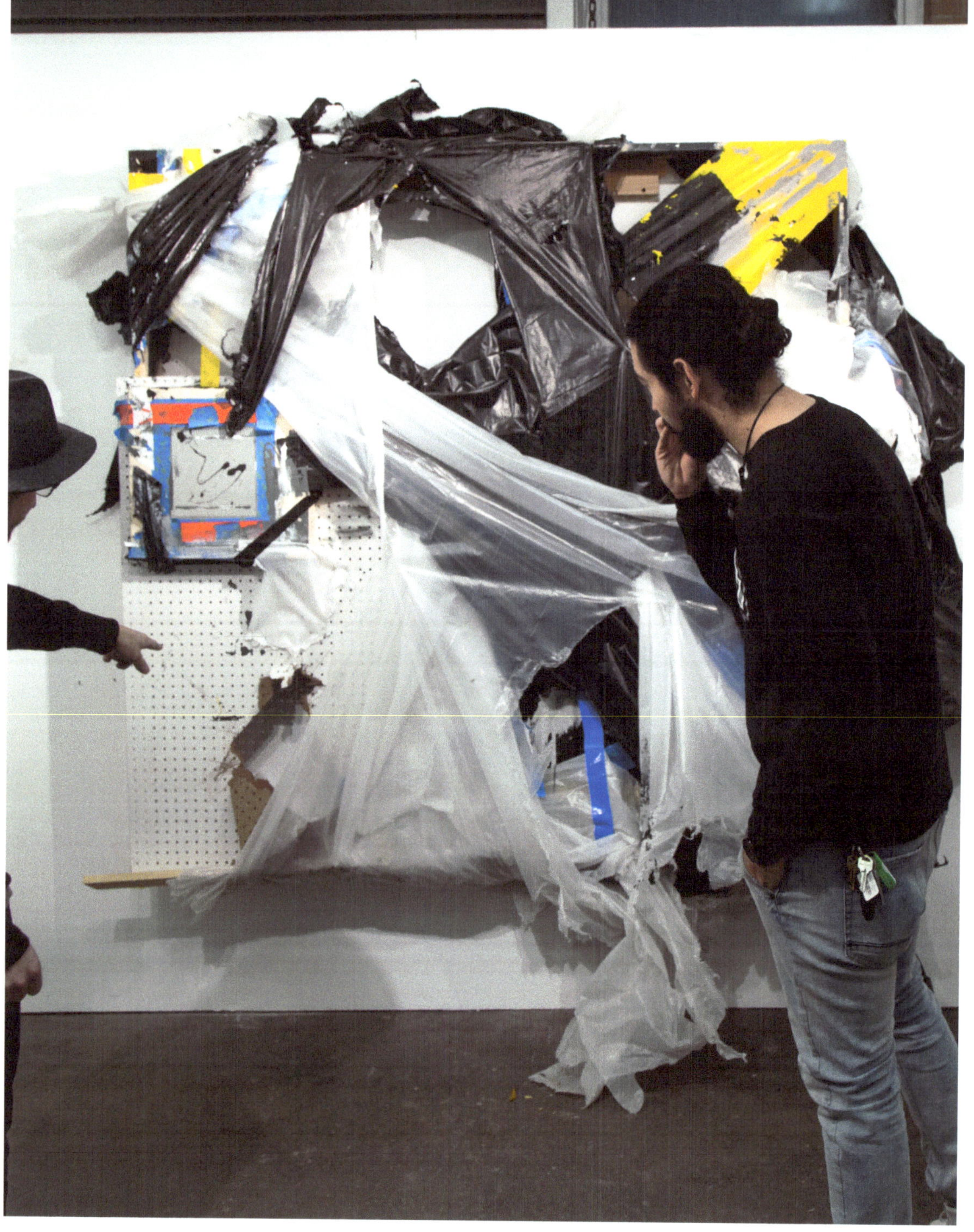

Chaos and Order

A Conversation with Joshua Reyes

Joshua Reyes creates large-scale paintings that explore the idea of "chaos and order". He uses non-traditional mediums such as tape, plastic tarps, and latex paint in an expressive way, reacting to the border of the piece.

Justin: Where did you begin? What got you into art?

Joshua: In high school, I took my first drawing class and my teacher really cultivated my skills. She said that I had something and told me that I should pursue art. I thought about it and was like, *I can draw in school? Yeah, I'm down*. Once I started college, I went through a period of time where I tried to make sense of majoring in art. I loved art because it's what brought structure and order to my life, but I wasn't sure if I should go through with being an art major. At some point, I realized that I needed to do it. I couldn't deny it.

I went into art school, and hated the first two years of drawing perspective, landscape, and the figure. I almost changed majors. During my junior year, they said "do whatever you want" and the whole world opened up to me.

Ty: In retrospect, was there anything invaluable that you learned in the two basic years that you originally hated?

Joshua: Yeah, I would say that. In order to make something good, you have to go through an allotted amount of time that you loathe. Once you get through that, something clicks and you make something amazing. For me, I never started out doing realistic things. I always got expressive. Gesture was amazing to me. Rendering movement instead of form was interesting to me. In every class I had, I became expressive and abstract.

I remember my instructor telling me that he could see that I used abstraction in my work, and that I was good at it. He told me that I couldn't do any of that for the rest of the semester. I had to draw figures realistically. It was torture. He told me that, before I made a mark on the paper, I had to look. Having to pause before I drew allowed me to render in a different way. It taught me how to look and see.

Ty: How does the process of looking and mark making relate to what you're doing today?

Joshua: It's directly related. A lot of what I'm doing today is about different approaches to mark making. It becomes all about tempo, rhythm, and composition. I think of my paintings more like songs. In a song, you can't play 1/8 notes the whole time. In some of my older paintings, I used a paint scraper and moved it across the canvas at different speeds. At a certain point, I step back and pause to look before I begin again.

Justin: So you're observing the mark that you made and finding a way to respond to it?

Joshua: Exactly. Before, it was all about expression. I never knew what the mark meant to the painting. It's all about actions that are reactionary to the previous action. It's intuitive, but at the same time, I'm implementing everything that I learned before like design, composition, balance, structure...formal things that I learned that are in my head that I'm not literally thinking about in the moment.

Ty: It's interesting hearing you talk about your work because I'm hearing all these different influences that are art related and not. You've mentioned music, and I think of William Kandinsky and how music was important for his paintings. You've talked about actions and science, and it reminds me of Newtons Laws of Motion. What are some of your influences and the way you think about art?

Joshua: Influences and experiences are something that I cannot deny. They are a part of me, and will always be a sub conscience component to who I am. Almost everything that I've learned in general is an influence to my work. To me, the most interesting part is when I can make the connections that are inside my art to the outside world. That's when you find more meaning to what you're doing, and you understand not only what your art means, but why you exist. That's the fascination: *Why am I here? What am I doing? How do I fit into the world?*

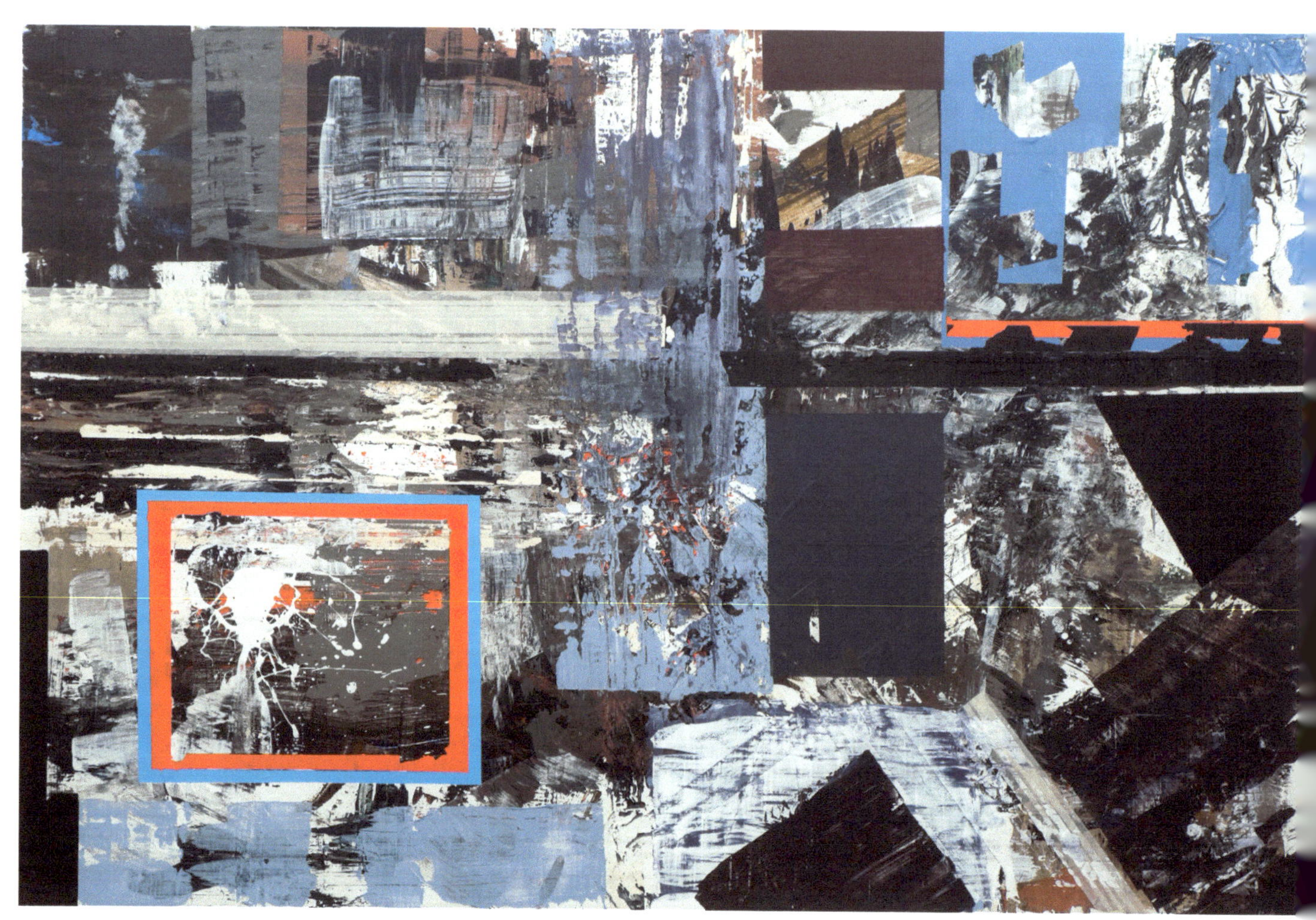

Joshua Reyes
Urban View, Arial Perspective
acrylic, gesso, tape on panel, 48 x 72in.

I do a lot of reading. I read a lot on philosophy, psychology, and I'm starting to read into linguistics. Communication is vital to humanity, and all I'm doing is communicating visually. If I can better understand how oral communication works, then I can better understand how to communicate visually. That's one of my interest.

Every action I make becomes like a word. I'm speaking to the object, and the object is listening. After I speak enough, I sit back and think about the meaning of the marks I made. Visual language exists to communicate. The communication my work gets to the outside world is based on the meaning I find in the works.

Ty: So you're saying that your process is a way of understanding yourself, and by doing that, you find better how you relate to the world in general?

Joshua: Exactly. It can't stop at me. I have to figure out why I'm doing this in the first place. It's fulfilling and way to understand myself. For me making art is the most personal and honest thing I do.

Ty: It's interesting that you say that. At the advent of Abstract Expressionism, Pollock's intention was to express emotions, but art critics looked at his work and said they were reflections of the time of the age he was living in. There seems to be correlations between your work and his work even though from an aesthetic standpoint they are very different. How do you see yourself in relation to what Jackson Pollock was doing?

Joshua. Jackson Pollock had amazing ideas and he did things that no one else was doing. At the same time, he denied the truth that he was a person from society. He wasn't trying to relate to people and was very introspective.

Justin: Like the Grinch in his cave?

Joshua: Kind of like that. He was genius in what he did, but he didn't acknowledged humanity. In this time period, I feel that it's irrational not to acknowledge humanity. That's why I like to share these ideas.

However, I would say that I am very influenced by Pollock. He was the the first abstract artist I studied. I was fascinated by the fact that he put it on the floor. He threw paint at it, he would step on it. He had a physical interaction with it. All of those ideas including expressing the the unconscious were the foundation for how I made art. I can't deny that Pollock was an influence.

Justin: The work you made until very recently was somewhat traditional. Now you're using non traditional mediums to make art. What made you decide to start using these materials?

Joshua: One of the critiques of my earlier work was that it always had a cityscape and industrial reference. There was this idea of industry and mass production. That led me to become more about construction and the idea of making things that are big and massive. This brought me to ideas of construction and made me more aware of the materials I use.

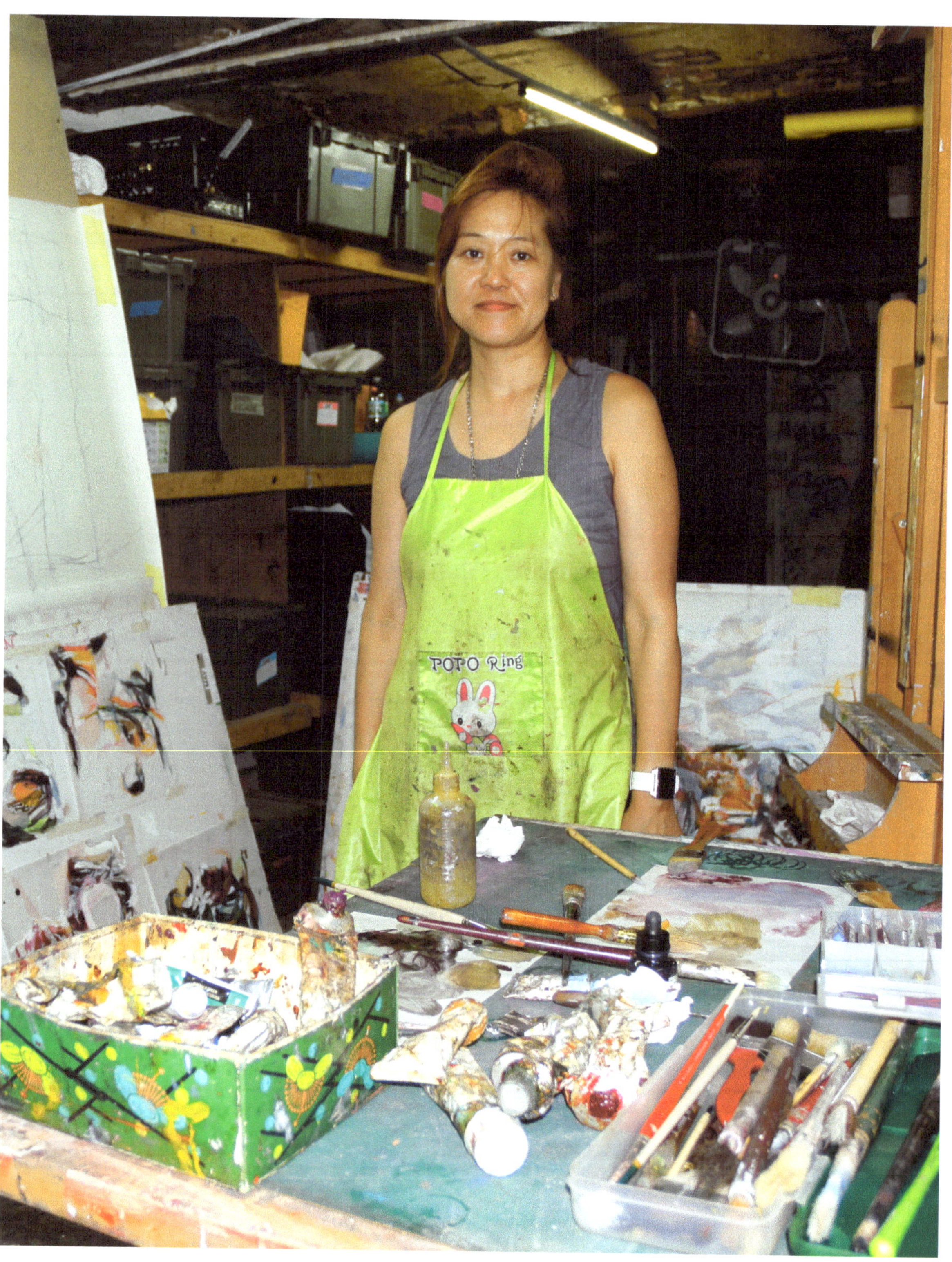
POTO Ring

Never-ending Paintings

A Conversation with Kayo Albert

Kayo Albert is an artist who lives and works in New York, NY. To create her abstractions, Albert uses a variety of mediums on mylar, a surface that is semi-transparent and made of polyester film. Ranging from very large to small, her works are layered, and it's impossible to take in the image at a quick glance. We began our conversation in her studio.

Justin: Would you mind starting off with a tour of your studio?

Kayo: Sure. Here's my studio space with is part of the Con Artist Collective that's located in the lower east side in New York. We are an artists community and I'm sharing a studio.

Justin: Did you go to school in New York?

Kayo: I did get a two year graphic design degree back in Kyoto. After that, I came to New York and studied painting. I went to three different schools included the School of Visual Art which is a very good school. I had good classes and connections from there.

Justin: So you decided to focus full time on being an artist rather than finishing school?

Kayo: Yes.

Ty: Did you start out in graphic design and then get into painting?

Kayo: Yes, I did.

Ty: Were you painting before you got into graphic design?

Kayo: Not intensely. I did a little bit of illustration, but that was about it.

Ty: I'm really interested in the mediums you're using. What interests you in using materials like mylar?

Kayo: I first discovered mylar from an exhibition I went to. The artist was drawing on it with oil pastel. I thought it was really interesting and refreshing, and I tried it myself. What I really like about mylar is that it is airy. If you hang it with some space between it an the wall, it has an open and semi translucent feel to it. That's one thing that I like about this material. Another thing I like is how easy it is to draw on it. My paintings are very involved with drawing. It starts and finishes with drawing.

Justin: What medium are you drawing with?

Kayo: Charcoal and pastel. The mylar is so smooth and these materials work well on it. If you draw on canvas, it doesn't give you the same clean fine line. That's why I continue working with mylar.

Ty: Your work is very layered. About how many lawyers do you work with?

Kayo: Multiple. As many as I can get until I'm satisfied. I like to overlap different colors to create a more interesting composition and deeper feeling.

Ty: I'm curious to hear more about the drawing aspects of your work. I know that landscape is very important for you, but these marks seem to be more intuitive. How do you decide what to draw?

Kayo: The important thing for me is movement. When you work on this big size, you have to physically move around the surface. It feels like a dancer moving their body. The movement evolves into something else like shapes and composition. I start from a place of calmness, and don't seek to express immediate emotions.

Ty: I think a lot of people are tired of that.

Kayo: Right. I want to go deeper than that. I take a deep breath and ask myself *where are you right now?* I start moving my hands and try to figure this out. I don't mean to say that my paintings show where I am exactly. That's how I start.

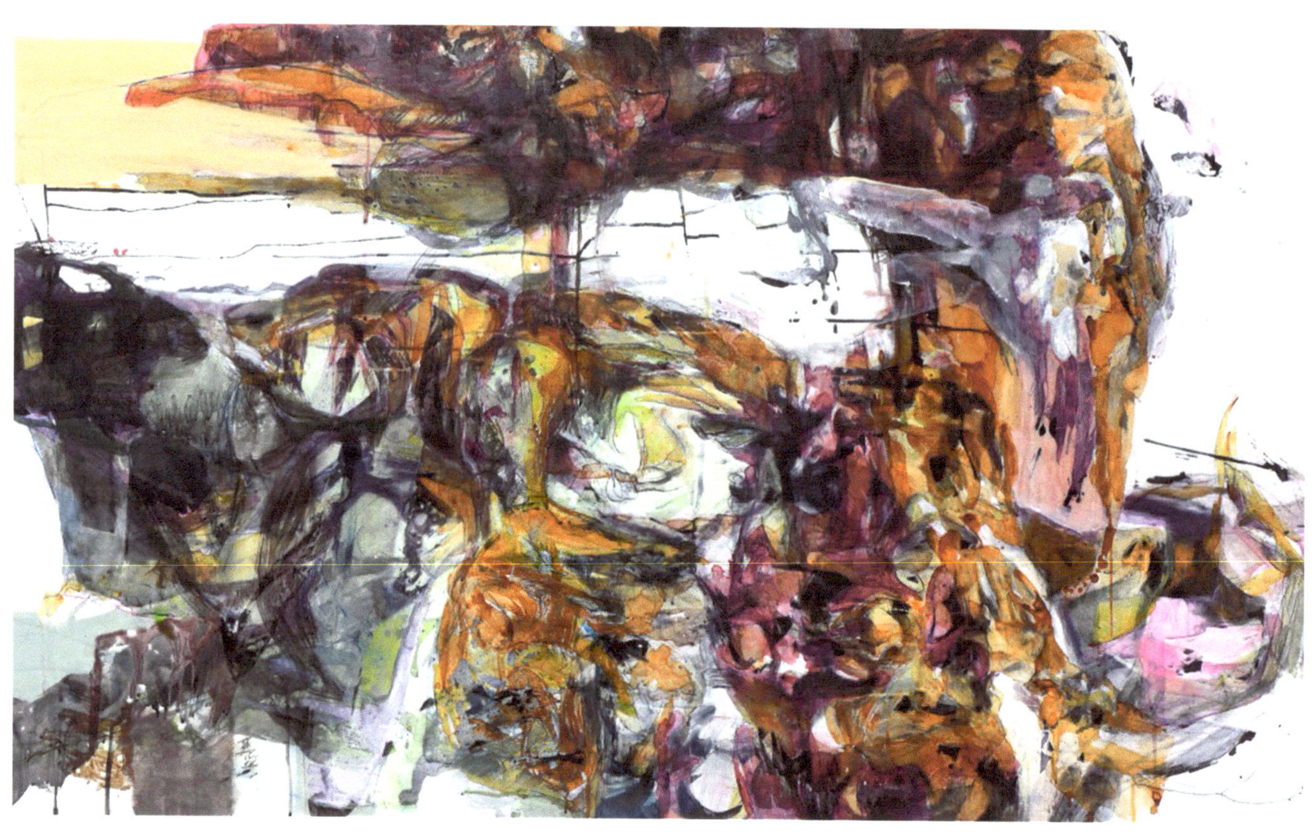

Kayo Albert
Emotional Landscape 1, 2016
charcoal, pastel, ink, oil, tempera, and acrylic on mylar, 42 x 70in.

Justin: You have an entire series titled *Landscape.* Would you say that these paintings are a reflection of an internal landscape or does it comes from references to actual landscapes?

Kayo: I don't mean to describe emotions as a landscape. It's more about what I paint gives the impression of a landscape. You can say they become a reflection of my internal landscape.

Justin: So you don't approach the painting with an image in mind, but your hands come up with it?

Kayo: Yes. It's not deliberate.

Ty: It seems that listening is a very imptortant part of your drawing process when you begin a painting by drawing. Once you start applying paint, does that process change or is it similar?

Kayo: I work in the same way. The process of drawing is different from how I apply color, but similar in the approach. The movement of my hand keeps going and evolves.

Ty: It appears that there is also drawing on top of the colors you apply. At what point do you decide to reincorporate the drawing?

Kayo: It's like drawing, then paint, and when the paint dries, more drawing and more paint.

Justin: So it's not a three-step process?

Kayo: No, my process is very continuous.

Justin: When viewing your work online, I can tell there's a lot there that I'm not able to see on the screen.

Kayo: Yeah, that's my goal. I want to make paintings where there's so much going on that you have to look at it for a long time and want to come back to because you always find something new.

Justin: That's translating in your work and it doesn't feel busy.

Kayo: That's something I have to keep in mind. Some people would say "oh, that's just too busy", but *I* can't help that. [laughs].

Ty: I notice that you have paintings that make use out of the entire composition, while you've left the background empty on others . When you're working, do you decide that you want to make less marks? How does that work?

Kayo: Because of the mylar, I do have this in mind. In some works, I want to leave space that is open and unpainted. That's because of the effect that it creates on the mylar. I also sometimes mount the mylar on wood which give a different effect. Mounted on the wood panel, you can still see the wood grain which gives a nice, organic feel. I'm currently working on a series of mylar mounted on wood panel.

Justin: In the works that the mark is more isolated, is this decided beforehand or is it something you decide while you're working?

Kayo: I call those paintings my *Flow* series. In that series, I particularly focused on the relationship between two or more shapes. By placing them together close or in distance, they create a different space.

Ty: What are the decisions you make when you apply color?

Kayo: What I'm interested in is the relationship between layering of drawing, colors, space, and movement on the mylar. They all interact together to create unique composition in mood and energy.

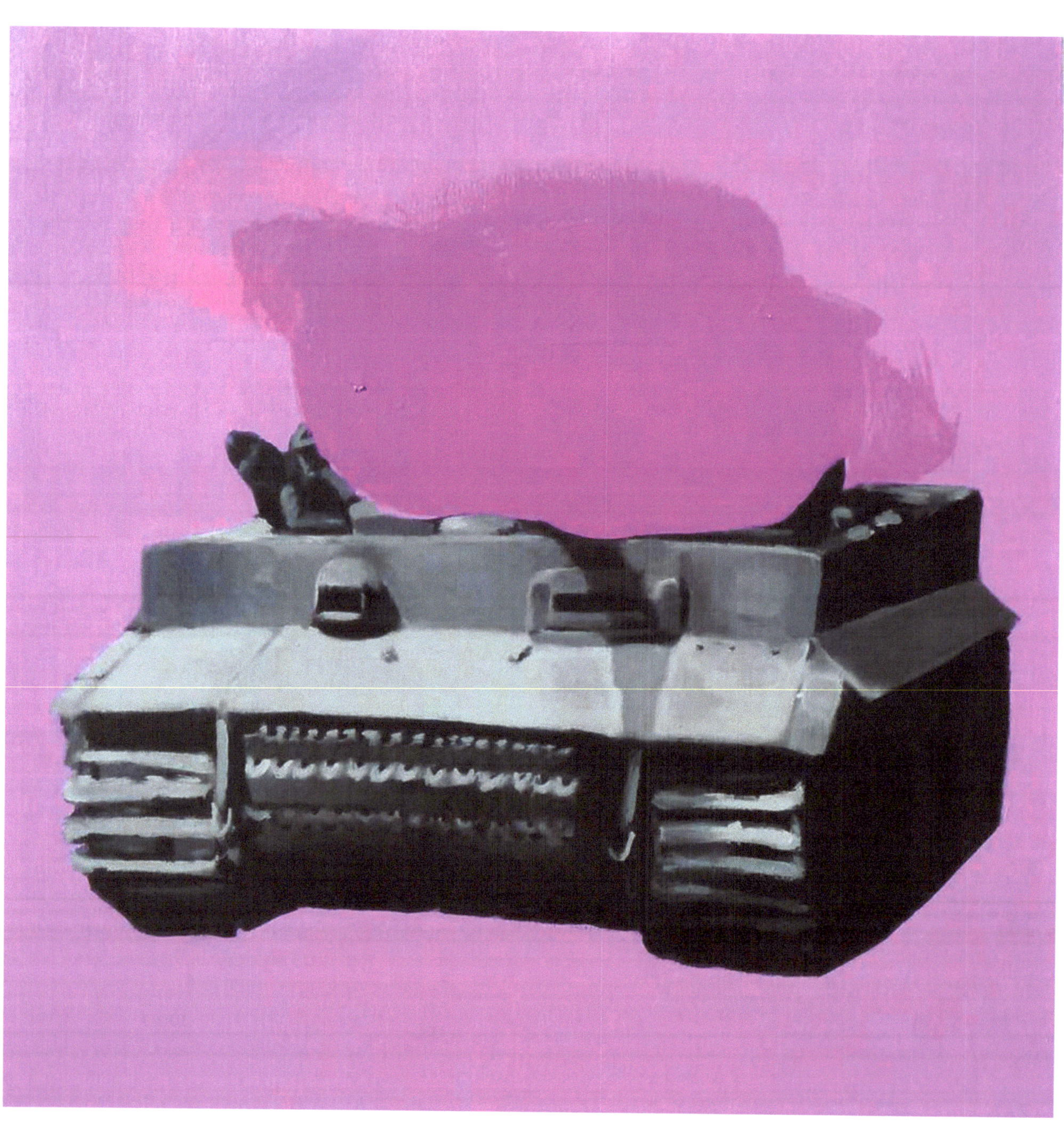

Evan Jones
On Tiger Mountain
acrylic on panel, 24 x 24in.

Painting History?
A Conversation with Evan Jones

Evan Jones is an emerging artist located in the Atlanta, GA. As an avid collector of WW2 photographs, Evans appropriates aspects of these images into his painting, questioning the idea of the inherent truth of photography and the role of painting as documenting history. His approach explores historical ideas related to photography and art theory.

Ty: At what point did art become something you wanted to pursue full time?

Evan: There was never a point that I decided to be an artist. This is just what I've always done. I was constantly drawing my whole life.

Ty: Where you always interested in the figure?

Evan: Yeah. The figures, objects, and human interactions with those objects. Specifically, I like WW2 technology and the advances in airplanes, tanks, etc.

Ty: So you're interested in both history and technology. What about your figures? Are they contemporary? Where do they come from?

Evan: I work with figures specifically from the WW2 era because it represents a turning point in world history. It fascinates me. I also work with some imagery from 9/11 which was also a turning point.

Ty: So in a way, referencing WW2 images and contemporary American history with 9/11 is a way of reimagining or processing history? What about those images are important to you and your work?

Evan: I'm not sure I know yet why they're important, other than that I keep coming back to them and I know there's something I'm digging at by depicting them. The process of combing through the imagery and figuring out ways to manipulate it in order to make it relevant to us today, not in a literal sense, but a broad human sense, is something I'm trying to do. Art has always been a lens to look at what has happened in history to humanity in a more subjective, emotional, or ethereal way. So I don't see what I'm doing by collecting and choosing to paint these images as any different than that. It's just adding on to their documentation.

Justin: What is your process in eliminating parts of the image? Do you have a narrative in mind?

Evan: There's a lot formal aspects that go into it and what will make a good image. I want to keep it general. It's about picking out things that will resinate with the viewer. For example, the piece that you feature in the Expo, Tojo Spills a Cup of Water, looks like he is sleeping, but this photo reference was taken after Tojo, the Japanese general in WW2, tried to kill himself.

Ty: It seems that the history painting genre dating back to the French Salon has some influence on your work. Do you see yourself as a history painter or are you dialoging about that?

Evan: Yes to both of those questions. The role of art throughout time has been to document and tell stories of past humanity. It switched pretty recently. You could argue that after WW2, painting became a cultural experience and much more intellectual for the artist. There's conceptual things after WW2 that weren't there before. WW2, maybe technology, open that up for artists. History painting wasn't as relevant anymore. It goes back further than that, but the post WW2 era broke it down.

Ty: What fascinates me about your work how you're referencing something that's historical and academic, but you're going about it in a total post modern way.

Evan: Right.

Ty: Found imagery is important to your work. You're not creating new images. I'm curious how post modern thought and artists like Richard Prince influenced your work.

Evan: Hugely. Richard Prince is one of my biggest influences. Like him, I would argue that I'm not really

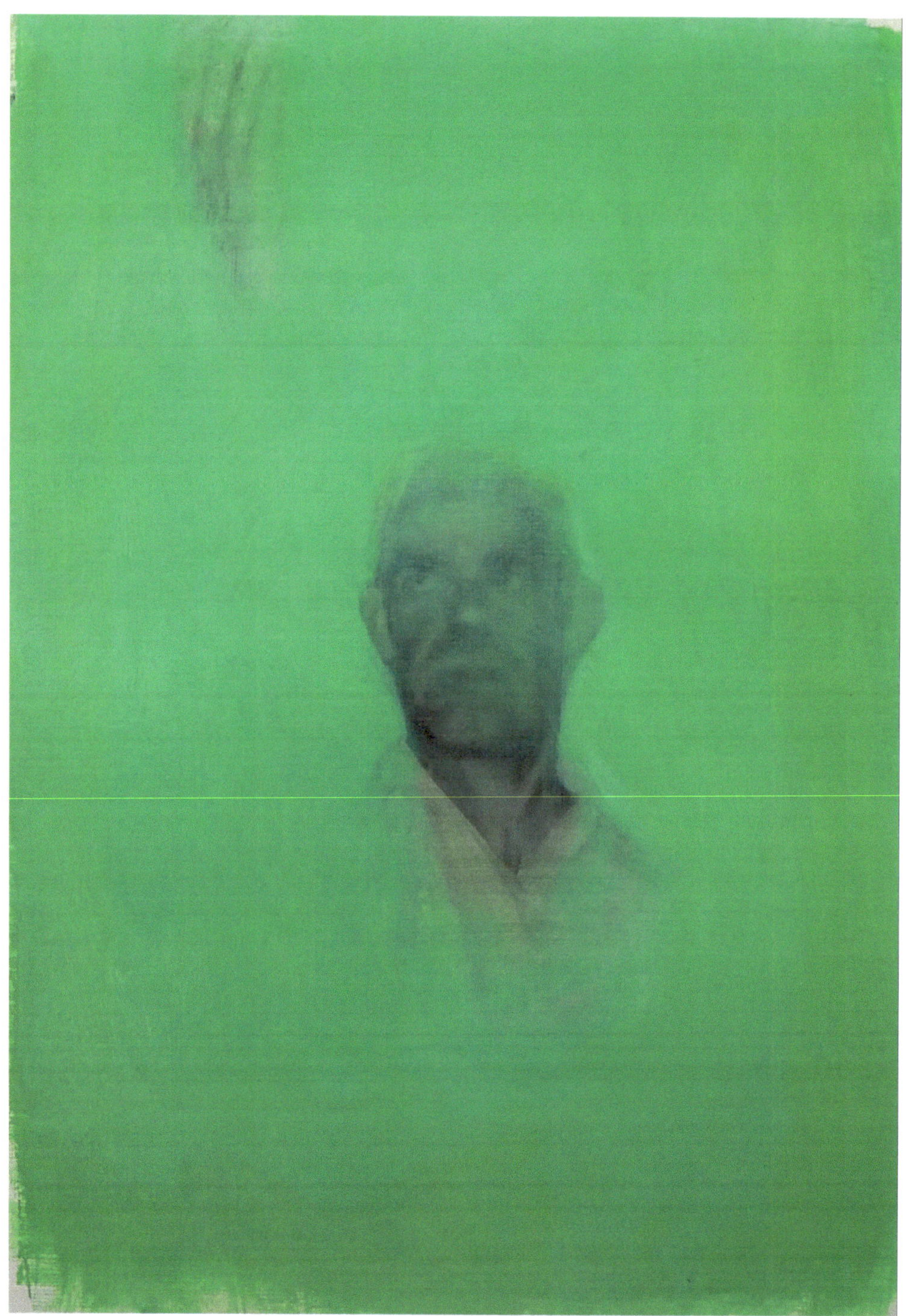

Evan Jones
Untitled, 2016
acrylic on paper, 12 x 9in.

interested in making things that come from me. I'm more interested in changing things that already exist. Prince addresses the myth of the cowboy, which in a 1,000 years will go away, but we're left with the imagery. Maybe Prince's cowboys will be what historians look at to try and figure out what we were all about. And I think that's funny because his cowboys aren't even original, but that says a lot about us, right?

When we look at history, we're looking at ancient Egypt and ancient Rome and the things they produced. We're left with the products of their thoughts. When I'm collecting imagery, the art happens as I sort through and process these historic images, thinking about it after the fact. With Richard Prince and artist like him, the idea of taking things from culture and processing through them is important for my work. I'm just going back a bit further because it raises some questions in my mind about when things stop being relevant, and when they become something that happened that we just learn about or see in pictures, versus something we actually "know" about?

Ty: Speaking of images, where do you find your images and what are some of the decisions you make when selecting them?

Evan: Books, internet...I'm constantly looking for them. I collect WW2 picture history books. It's interesting because a lot of the books use the same images, but crop them and scale them up or down that makes it seem like the image is unique. I choose the images formally and what will make a good painting. I take this image, tweak it in some ways, and then put it back in the world.

Justin: It's interesting that you add your personal experience o the photography.

Evan: That's actually something I haven't thought about, but is pretty fascinating. What happens when you replace the means of documenting history with conceptual ones? Interesting.

Ty: The way you're interpreting is interesting also. The history of war photography, the way the image was taken was manipulation in and of itself. During the Civil War, dead bodies were staged for photographs. You manipulating the images seems to unravel this. Is that correct or is it more that you are doing?

Evan: You nailed it. Is what I'm doing any different than lining up bodies on a Civil War battle field? Is that any different from what I'm doing with taking images and placing them on a colored background? I don't know.

Justin: All the figures in your painting are black and white. I'm curious to hear about your decision behind this.

Evan: For the black and white images, it's about staying true to the original image. I want to keep the history.

Ty: There's a lot of narrative behind your work. Even from a formal perspective that can be seen. You also include some gestural, quick sketches in your work. I'm curious to hear more about those.

Evan: They have a lot to do with technology. I started out by making these really quickly in photoshop. I would find the image, erase parts of it in photoshop. I would then add back in sections of the images with formal, gestural marks. These marks would replace the history data of the image.

Ty: So it's a way of humanizing history, in a sense?

Evan: Yeah. It's about thinking about the role of art in history. Is art still trying to document history?

Justin: And is art manipulating history?

Evan: Yeah.

Justin: It's interesting how you replace the technology in the photography, with a more conceptual form of technology by using Photoshop.

The FOA Winter 2017 Expo showcases the work of ten emerging artists from across continents. Ranging from Texas to England, oil paint to textiles, abstraction to representation, the artists selected for this expo are extremely varied. The different places they work from in the world only accentuates this. Though distinct, a unifying principle between these artist is their commitment to explore personal aesthetics based on historical ideas of art. Each of these artists shares the spirit of "making it new", whatever that means for their medium and concept.

Winter Expo

2017

Kayo Albert

Savonna Nicole Atkins

Sabre Esler

Betsey Gravatt

Andrew Indelicato

Evan Jones

Christina Macal

Jen Oldknow

Joshua Reyes

Shelby Rogers

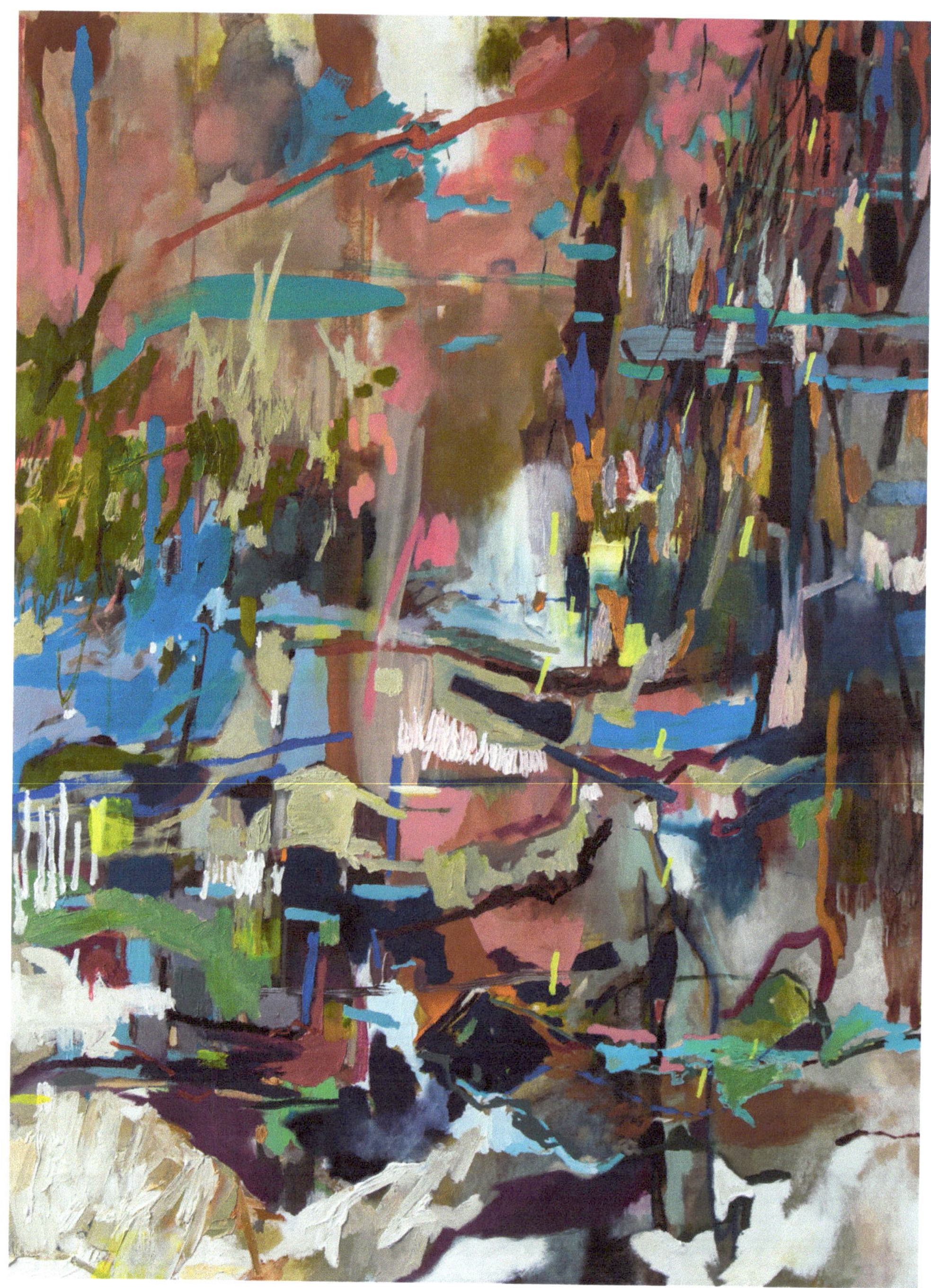

Savonna Nichole Atkins
Just A Little Bit More Purple, 2015
acrylic, graphite, pastel, and oil on panel, 53 x 40in.

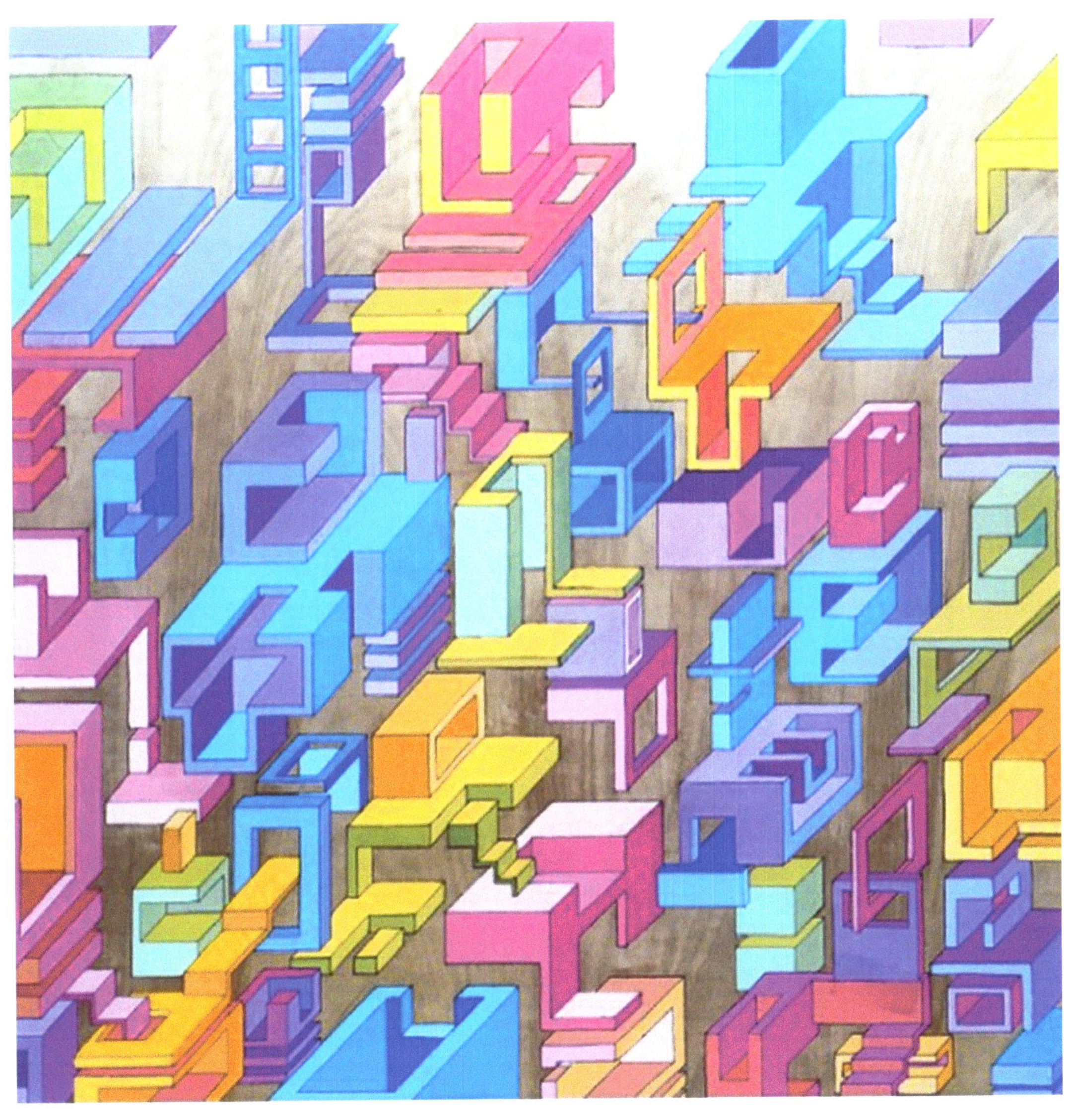

Betsey Gravatt
Dream Recipe, 2015
gouache and ink on birch, 24 x 24in.

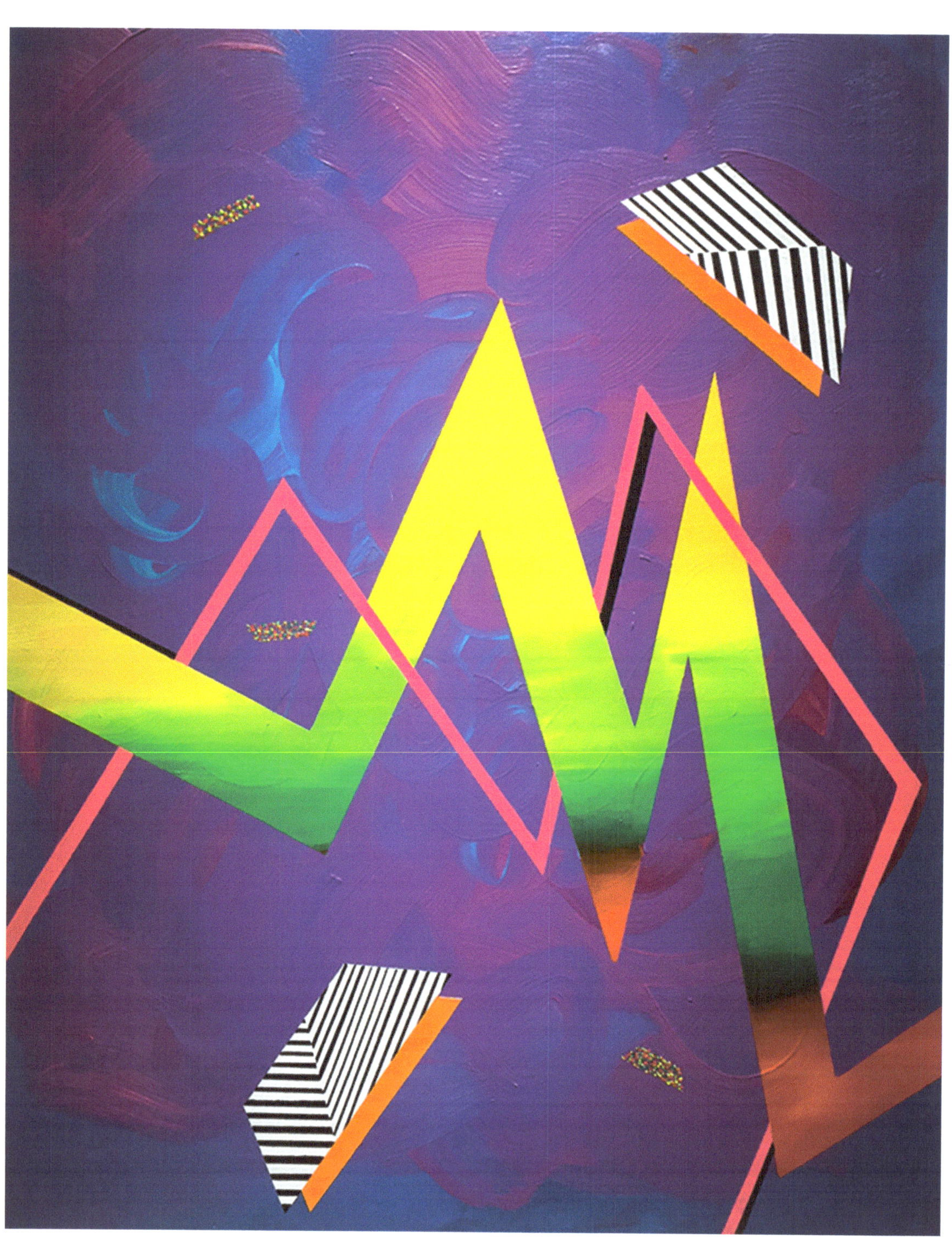

Andrew Indelicato
Array Formation, 2016
acrylic on panel, 16 x 20in.

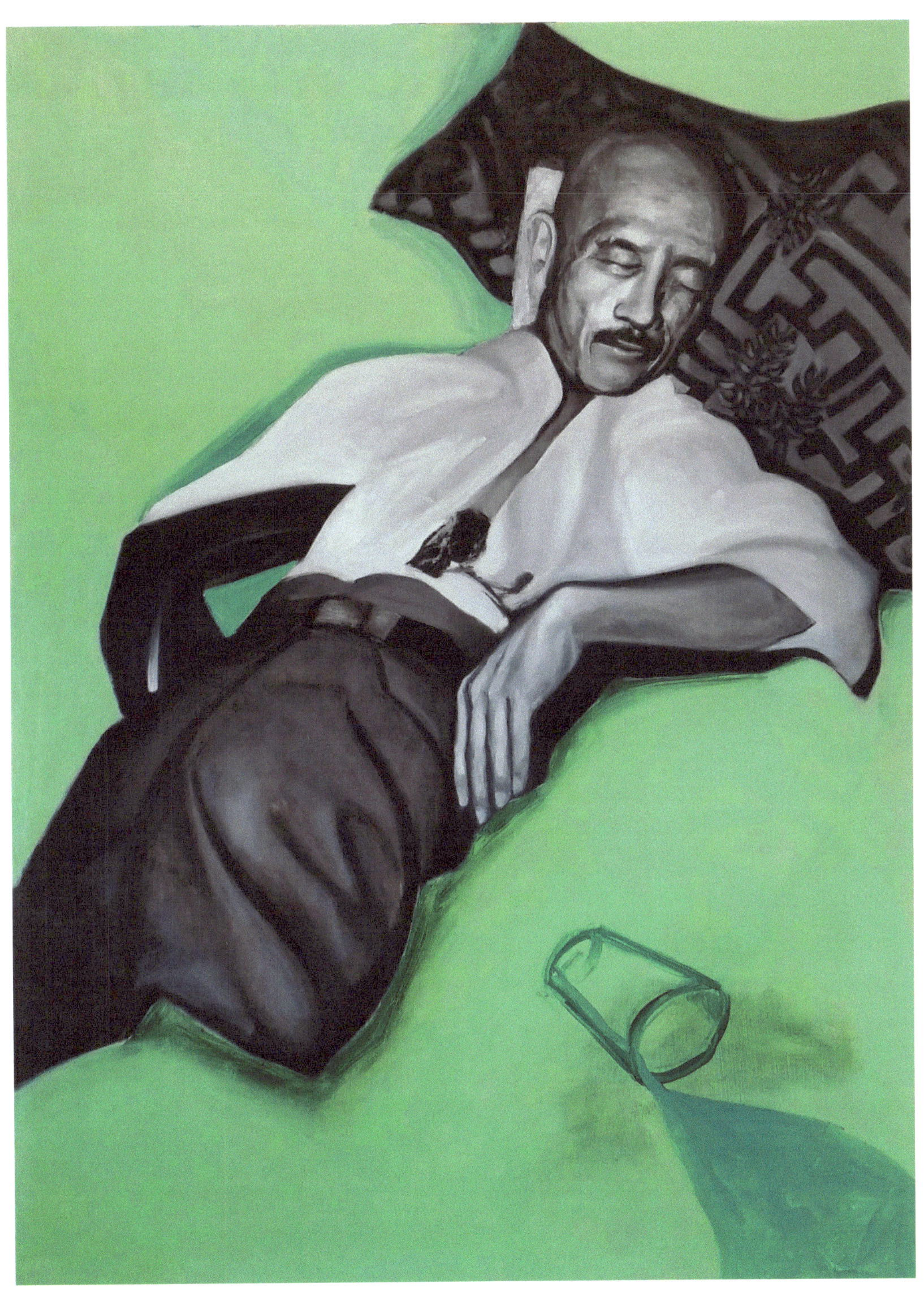

Evan Jones
Tojo Spills A Cup of Water, 2016
oil on panel, 48 x 36in.

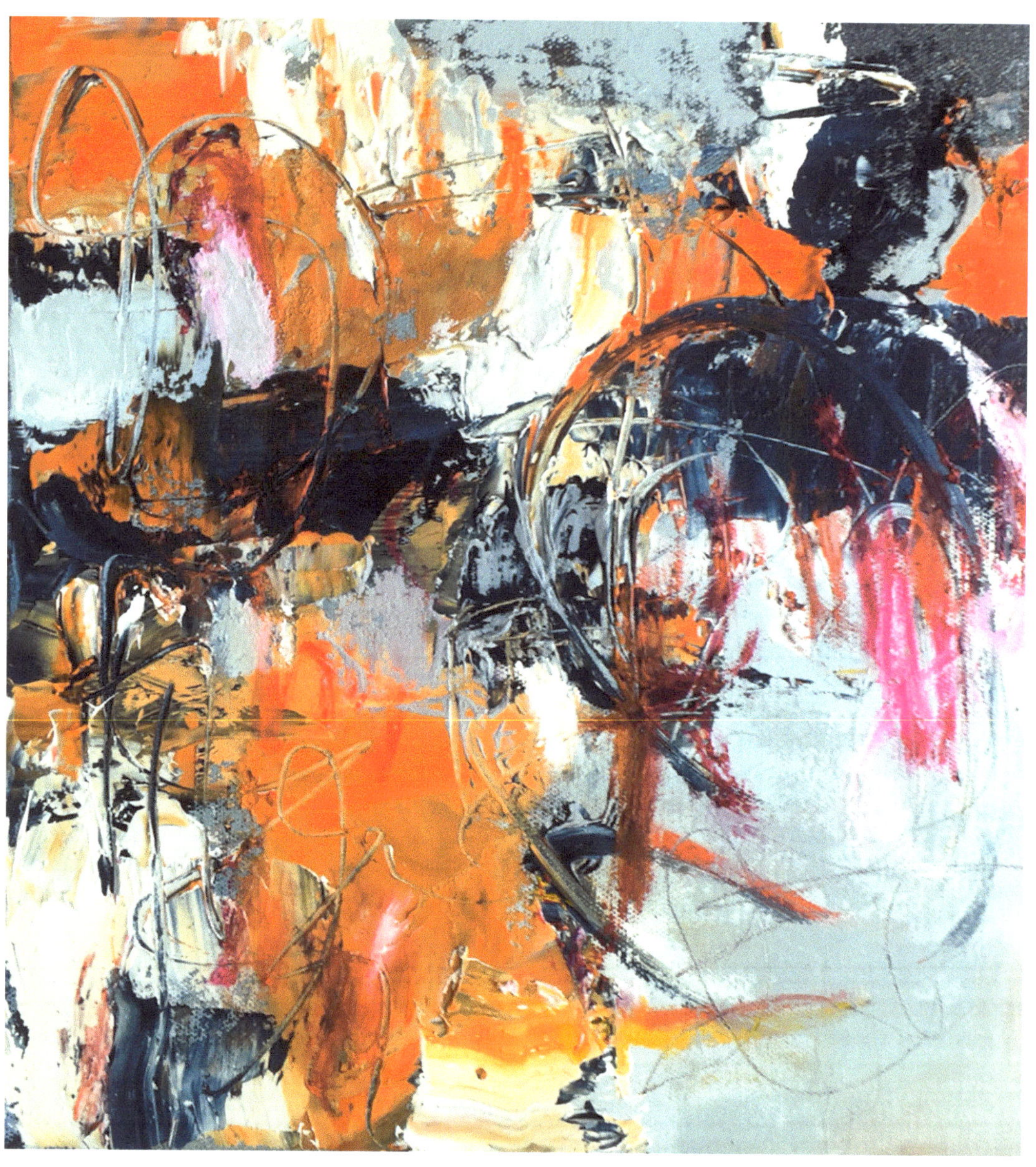

Jen Oldknow
Small Treasures 4, 2016
oil and wax on canvas, 12 x 12in.

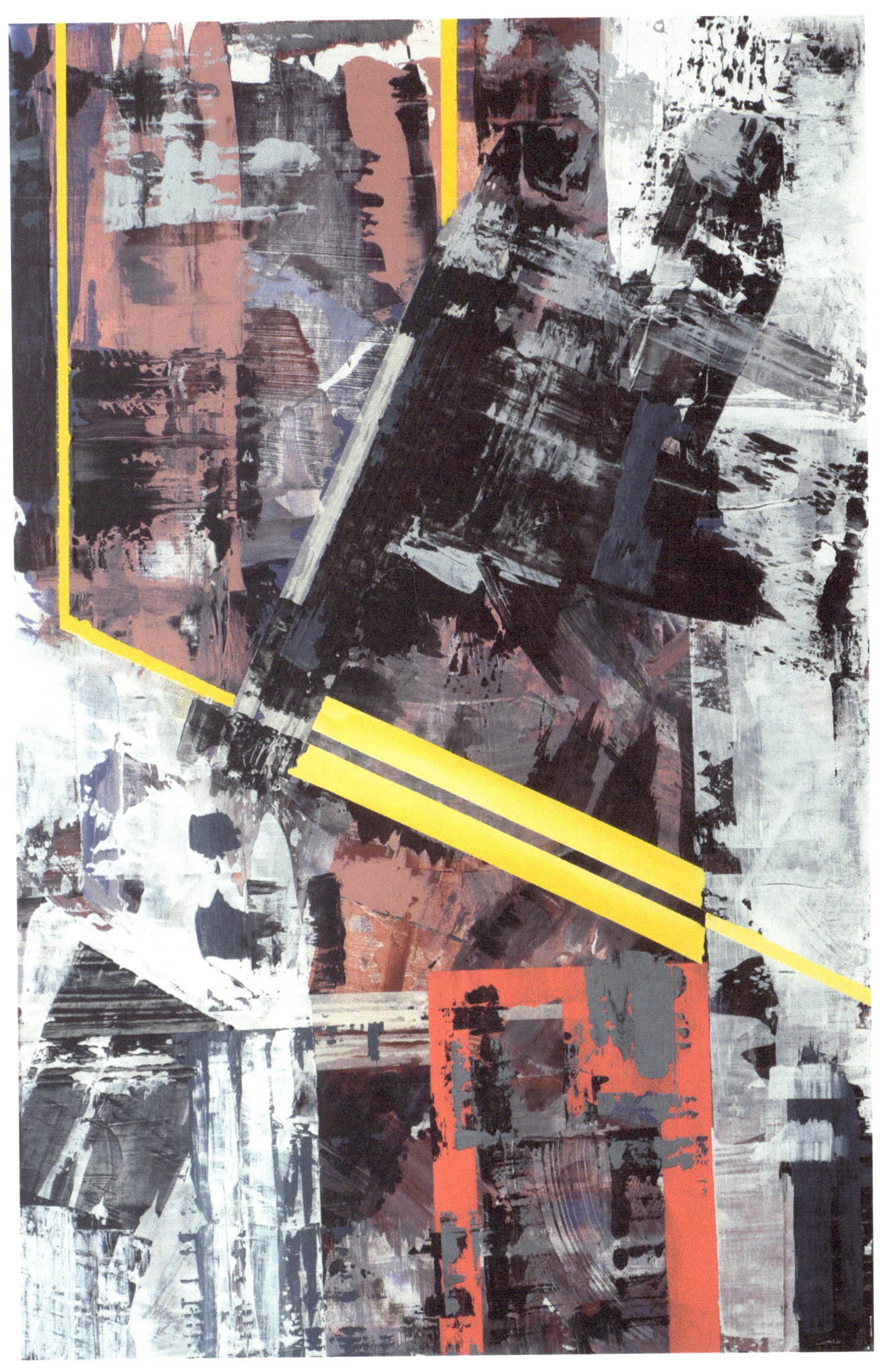

Joshua Reyes
This Line Marks the Cityscape, 2015
acrylic, gesso, tape on panel, 72 x 48in.

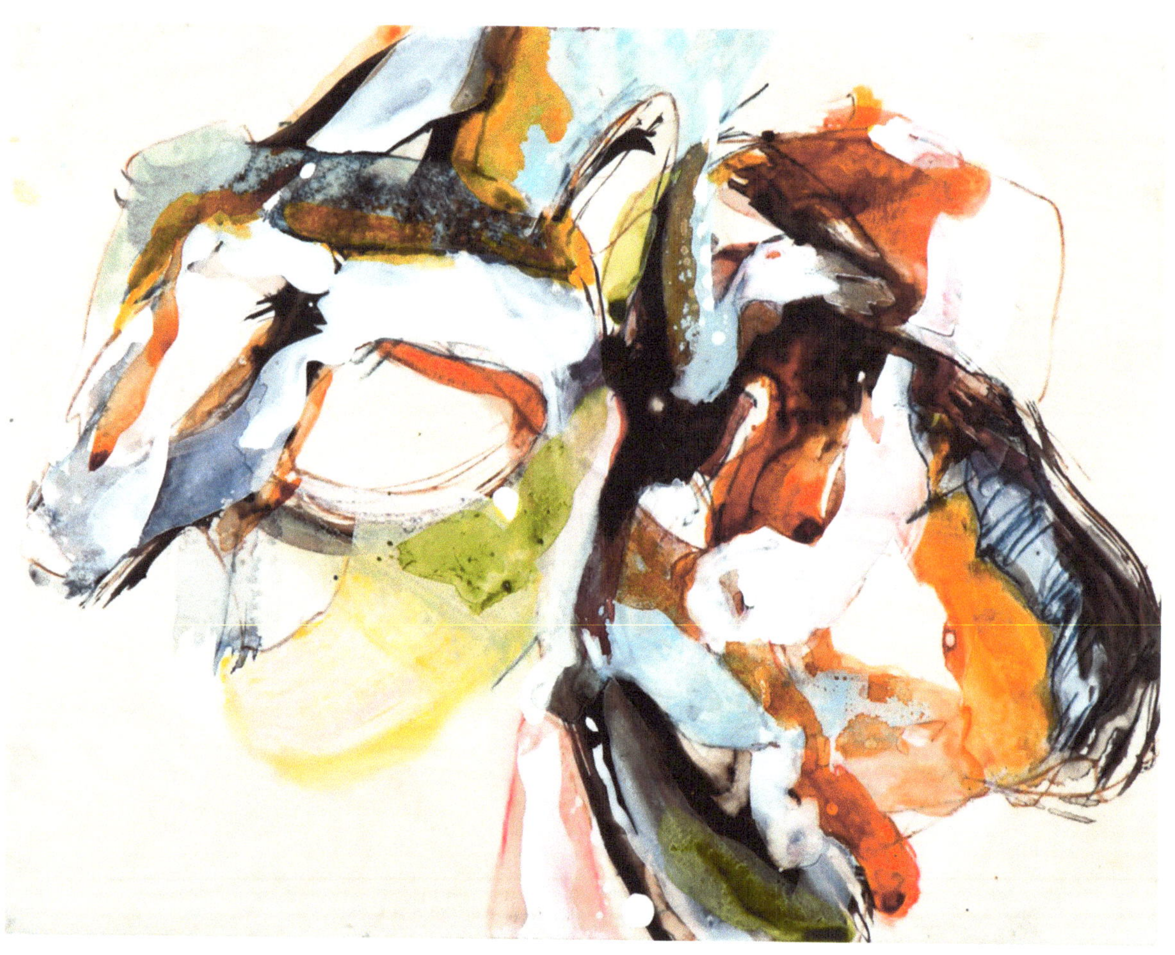

Kayo Albert
Flow 3, 2016
charcoal, pastel, ink, oil, tempera, and
acrylic on mylar on panel, 12 x 16in.

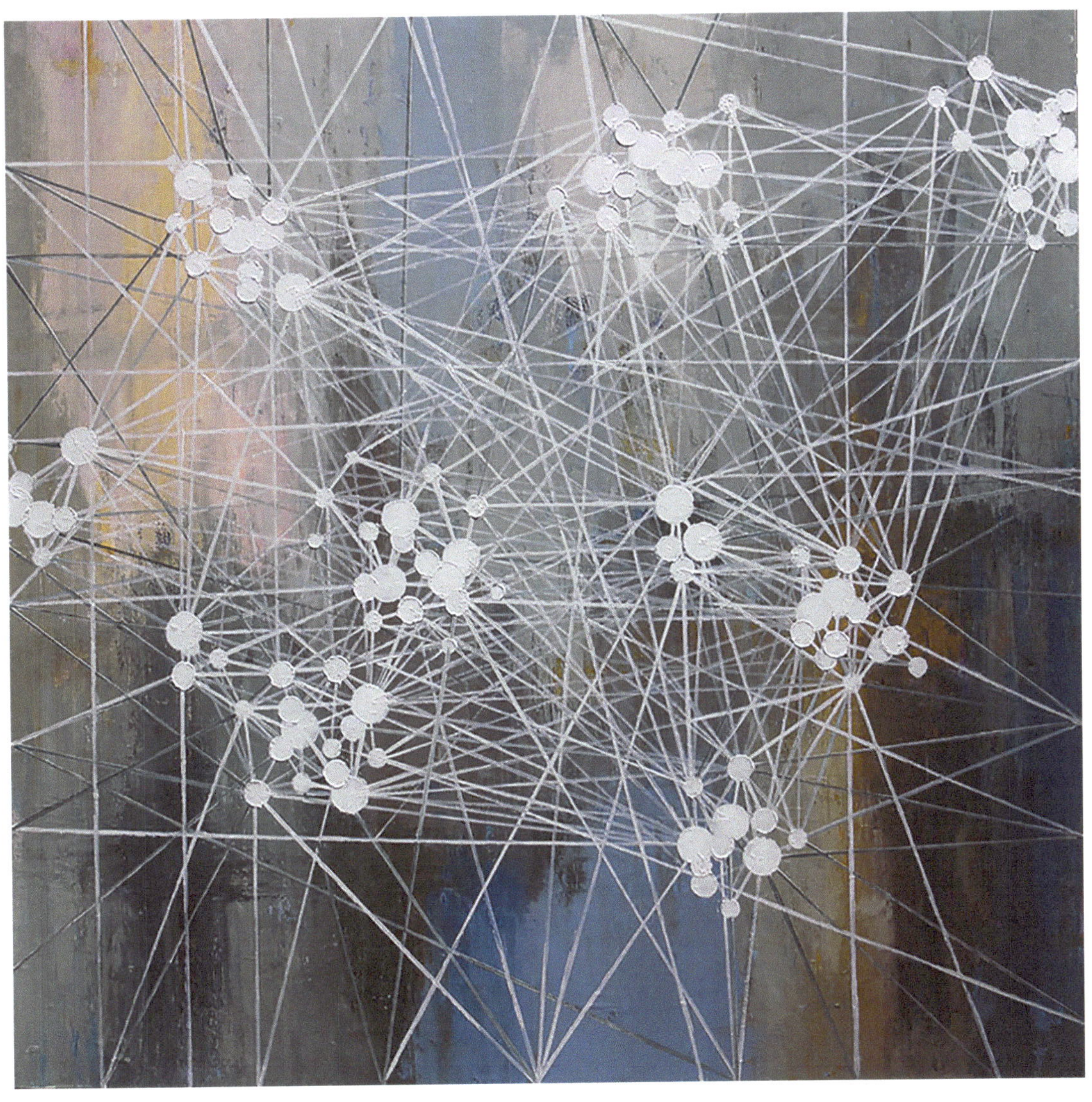

Sabre Esler
Complex Correlations, 2016
oil on canvas, 30 x 30in.

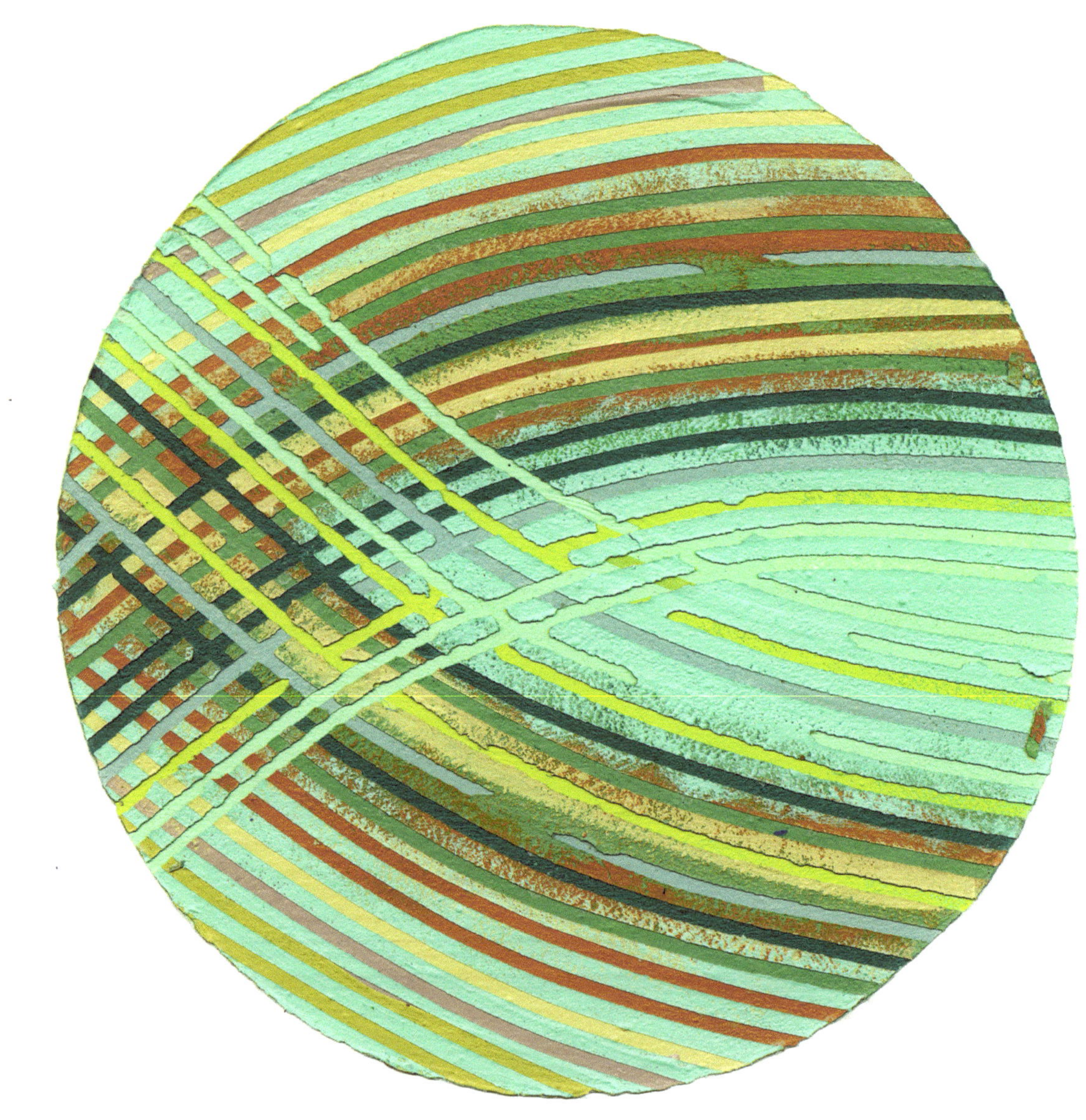

Christina Macal
Circle Paintings #11
acrylic on paper, 11 x 17in.

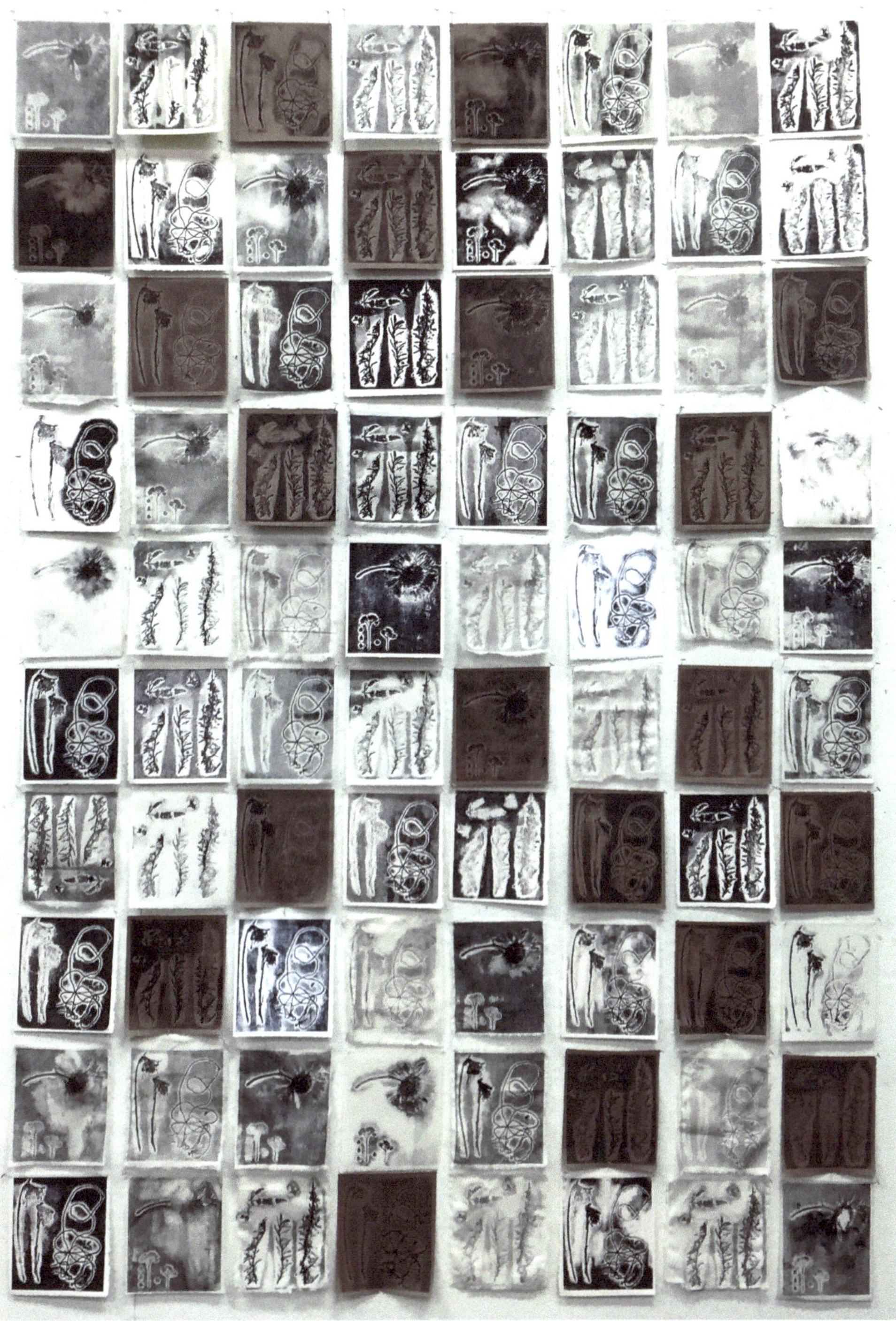

Shelby Rogers
Colograpgh taxonomy (installation), 2016
archival ink on paper, 80 x 53in.

Kayo Albert
New York, NY

kayoalbert.com

Deeply influenced by Carl Jung and Abstract Expressionism, I am interested in connection with people in subliminal level. I imagine having invisible rhizome nourished by memories dreams, flashes of images and ideas stored deep under the ground which is connecting with others to share emotion or beauty regardless of locale, age and race.

Painting is for me is a journey to my rhizome, to discover how all my perception and experience have blended. It is then drawn to construct almost emotional landscape because it is built on structure, movement and special composition.

Drawing is essential in my work which allows me to dig deeper, moving through the surface tracing movement and creating depth. Painting with oil, ink and other water based paints creates various reactions and effects. These lines and paints overlap to reveal all my process without erasing them. The physicality of drawing and painting, in immersing my whole body in the work is fundamental; it also gives audience to experience the sense of being drawn into the piece.

Mylar provides great surface for drawing and its lightness, luminosity and airiness is like no other.

When mounted on wood panel, its' grain can be seen through the blank (unpainted) surface to create refreshingly organic effect.

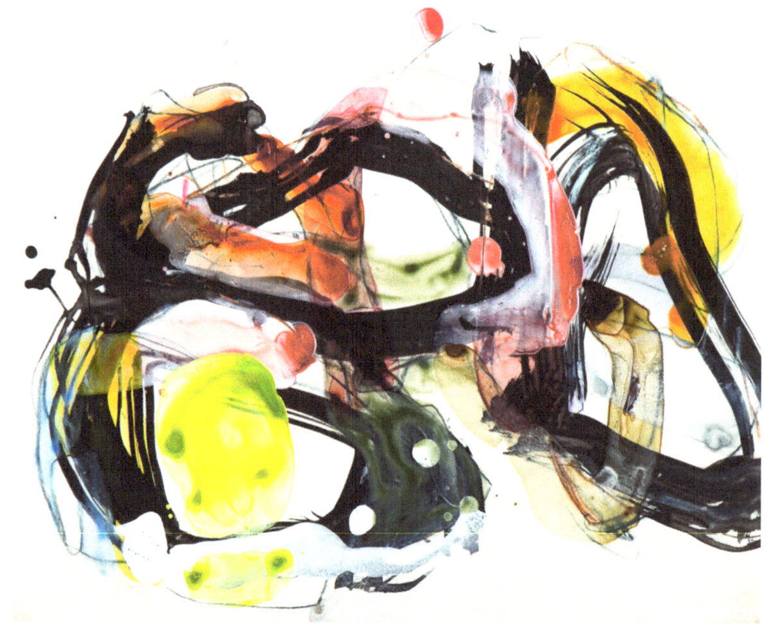

Kayo Albert
Flow 2, 2016
charcoal, pastel, ink, oil, tempera, and acrylic on mylar on wood, 11 x 14in.

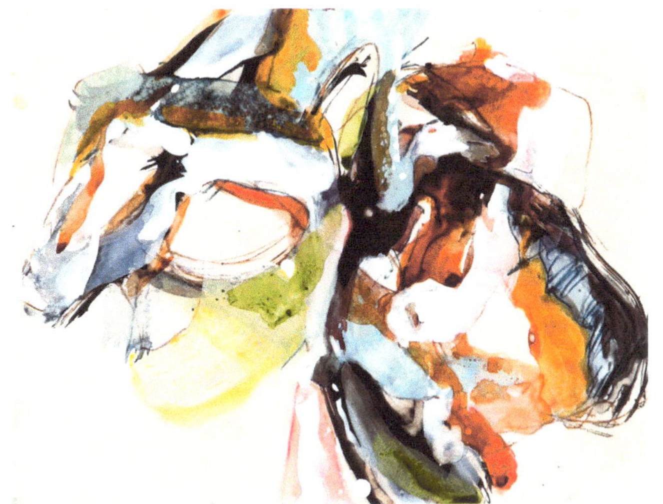

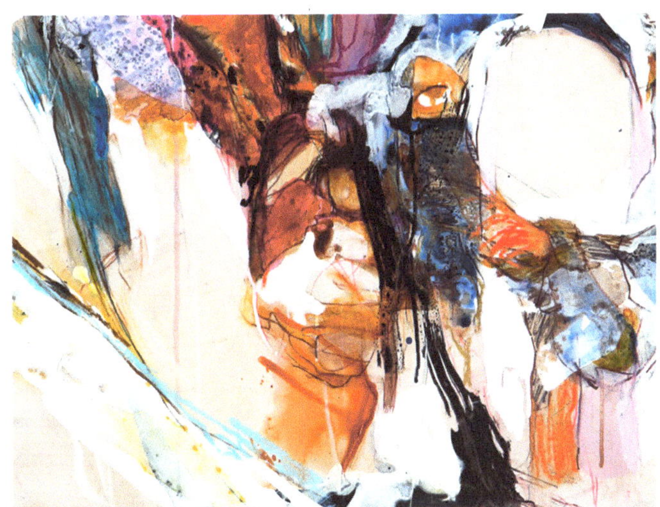

Kayo Albert
Flow 3, 2016
charcoal, pastel, ink, oil, tempera, and acrylic on mylar on panel, 12 x 16in.

Kayo Albert
Flow 6, 2016
charcoal, pastel, ink, oil, tempera, and acrylic on mylar on panel, 18 x 24in.

Savonna Nicole Atkins
Atlanta, GA

savonnanicole.com

Through abstract paintings and embroidered textile work, I explore self-concept and competition for social validation. I weave paint and sculptural marks into compositions fueled by personal memories and imagined landscapes. My obsessive tendencies speak through layers of detailed stitching, linework, brushstrokes, and fabric. Forceful marks, sheer washes, and delicate embellishments intertwine and collect with persistent intensity.

Stitches are sculptural lines that integrate and create strong securing connections. Whereas paint is more exclusively reserved for decoration and art, fabric is all around us and it is tied to everyday life and social circumstances. My hands cut and place fabric like smears and strokes of paint, relishing in the vast variety of textile textures. The craft of embroidery has evolved through the centuries, but it has remained an activity linked to decoration and self-improvement. The process involves patience, mastery of technique, and creative expression. Whether displayed on a dress or in the home, a piece of embroidery signifies care and cultivation. My embroidered textile pieces explore the desire to improve the self to an obsessive level. Embroidery becomes competitively complex. The pieces are elaborate accumulations of fabric and thread that involve great patience and dedication.

My work consistently joins tangible, physical processing with abstract, mental processing. The competitive struggles and absurdities of society feed the physical actions of making. I think of my work as existing in a realm between landscape and portrait; they are artifacts influenced by the messiness of human character and environment.

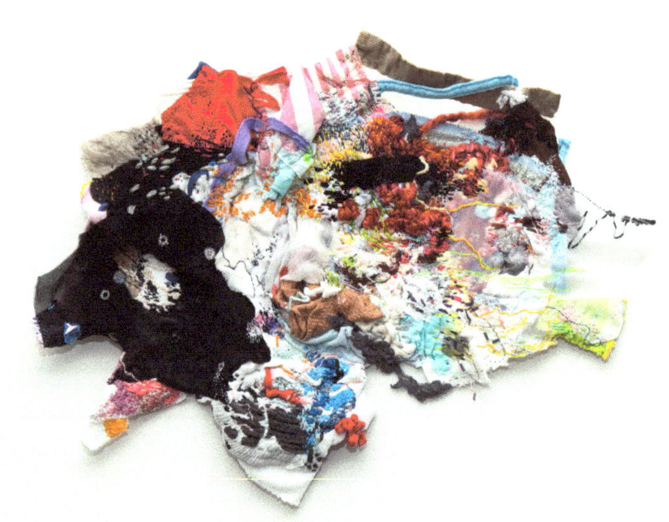

Savonna Nichole Atkins
Magnolias, Magnolias, Magnolias, 2016
fabric, thred, and beads, 15 x 20in.

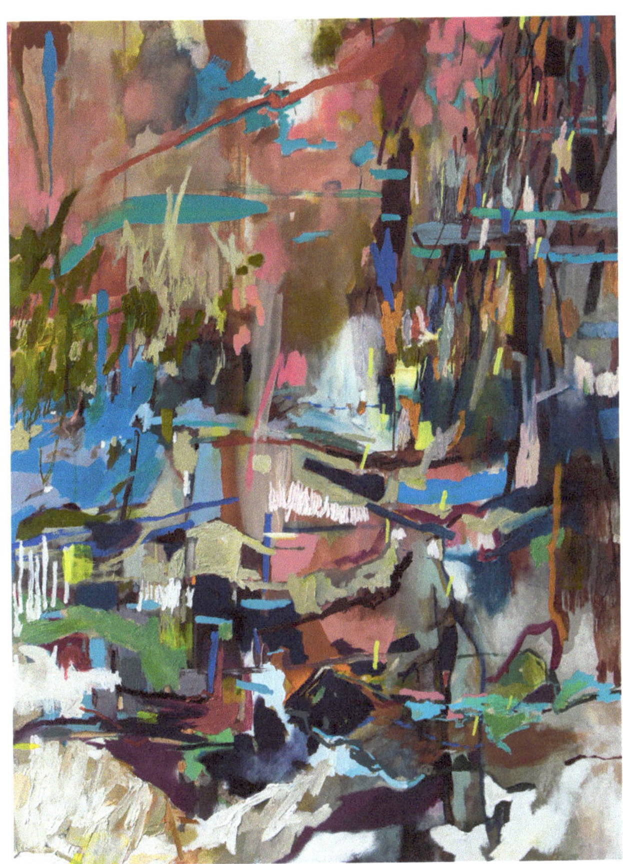

Savonna Nichole Atkins
Just A Little Bit More Purple, 2015
acrylic, graphite, pastel, and oil on panel, 53 x 40in.

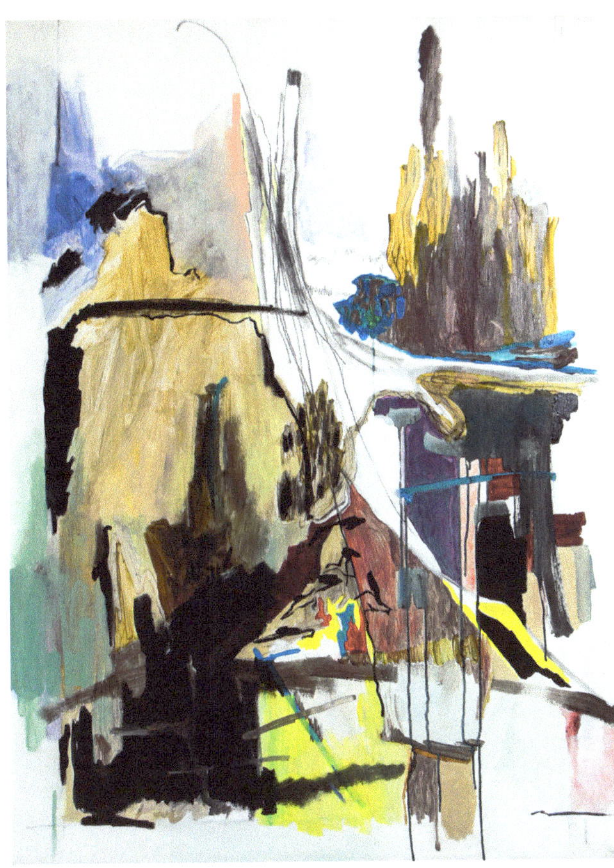

Savonna Nichole Atkins
Lemon Squeeze, 2014
acrylic, graphite, pastel, and oil on panel, 53 x 40in.

Sabre Esler
Atlanta, GA

sabreesler.com

My work explores the architecture of thought and mental structures created in problem solving. Architectural patterns, scientific graphs, neural receptor pathways; combining predictable patterns and breaking them, these are concepts that I think about when making work. I create a visual format for seeing the unseen, exploring the riddle of personal truths based on perceptions and paradigms. This work began while researching my thesis at SCAD. Patterns of thought can be interpreted as complex mathematical hierarchies, that may weave endlessly, creating an looping patterns. My focus is the relentless pursuit of the human spirit to solve problems.

My process embraces seeking the unknown and gaining a new discovery. My working practice is to fabricate a sculpture that showcases an aspect of thought patterns. A recent body of work uses mapping of the molecular networks for neuron function in the brain during PTSD episodes. From a sculpture, I create paintings and prints, which could be interpreted as residual after affects of a real event, much like a memory. This practice allows me to continue to change, adapt and explore the patterns and create hierarchies through layering techniques. I explore combining painting and printmaking or painting and sculpture to create hybrid pieces. By combining materials and practices, I am experimenting, much like a scientist does when exploring hypotheses. The result is to seek a greater understanding of the complexities of the human condition, which is both universal, and yet unique and personal to the individual

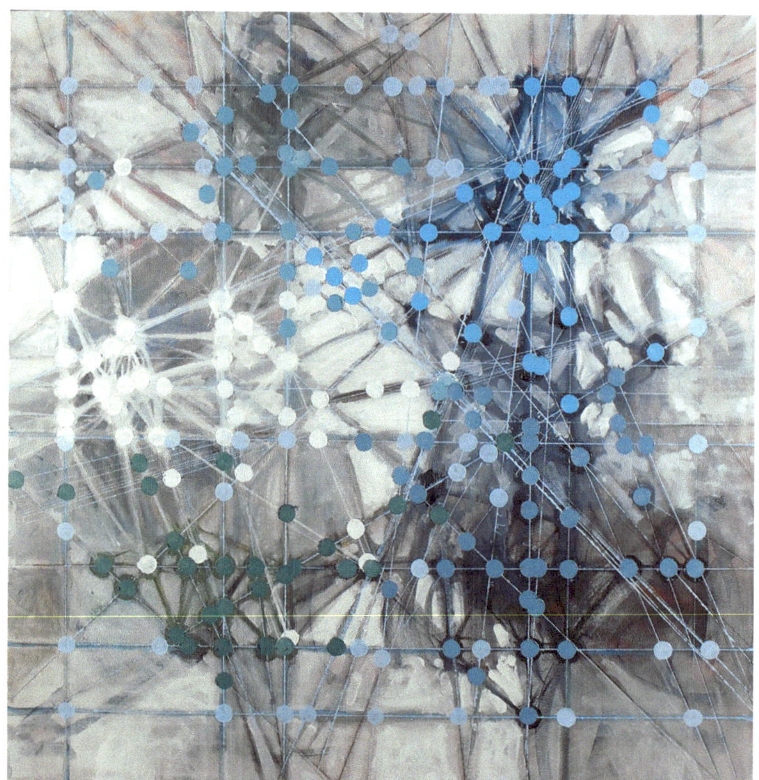

Sabre Esler
Evolution of an Idea, 2016
oil on canvas, 48 x 48in.

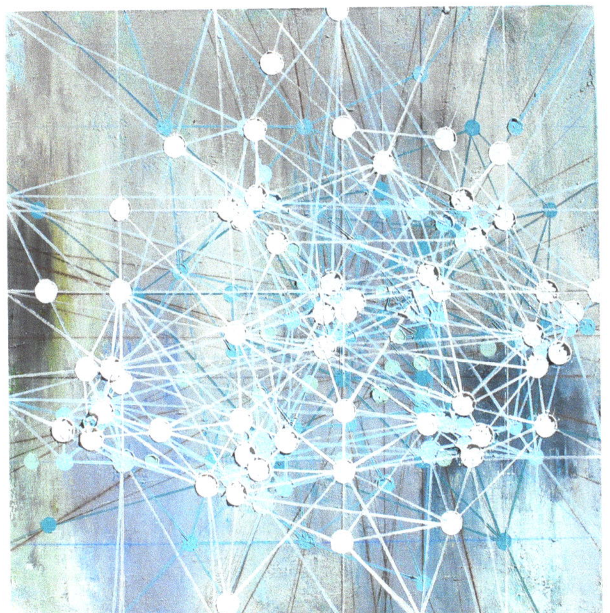

Sabre Esler
Crystalized II, 2016
oil on canvas, 30 x 30in.

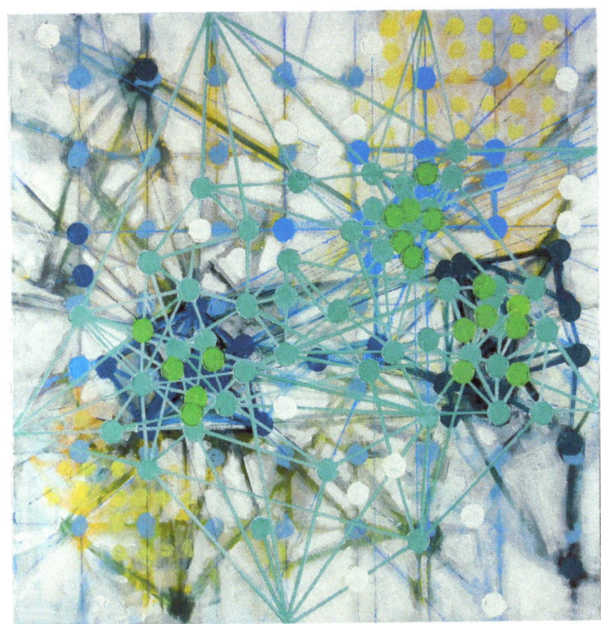

Sabre Esler
Multiplicity, 2016
oil on canvas, 30 x 30in.

Betsey Gravatt
Denton, TX

betseygravatt.com

In my sculptures and paintings I tend to use over the top, bright colors that I associate with happy memories, as well as toys or cartoons I liked as a child. I am inspired by children's toys that were popular in the 90's, such as Lisa Frank and Polly Pocket dolls, as well as TV shows I watched as a young girl. By using colors and shapes inspired by 90's pop culture, my paintings and sculptures can appear inviting and attractive at first glance, however, the reoccurring amorphous blob forms and synthetic materials can also be seen as grotesque.

Growing up in very rural areas of North Carolina and Texas, I have always been fascinated with the ways people adapt to and live in urban and rural settings. Location has always been incredibly influential in my body of work, and I find that my surroundings and environment alter and shape my artwork. As well as taking influence from 90's pop culture, the content of much of my work is inspired by crowded cities and rural landscapes. I am interested in the harsh contrast between these types of environments, which I attempt to illustrate non-representationally, through color, shape, and line.

My paintings are exploratory rather than didactic, and one of my goals is to create another reality for myself and my viewers to explore, that appears to be friendly and playful, but upon further investigation can start to seem ambiguous or unsettling. I attempt to evoke confused feelings of happiness and disgust by combining non-traditional media such as expanding foam, string, plastic, and glitter with traditional drawing and painting.

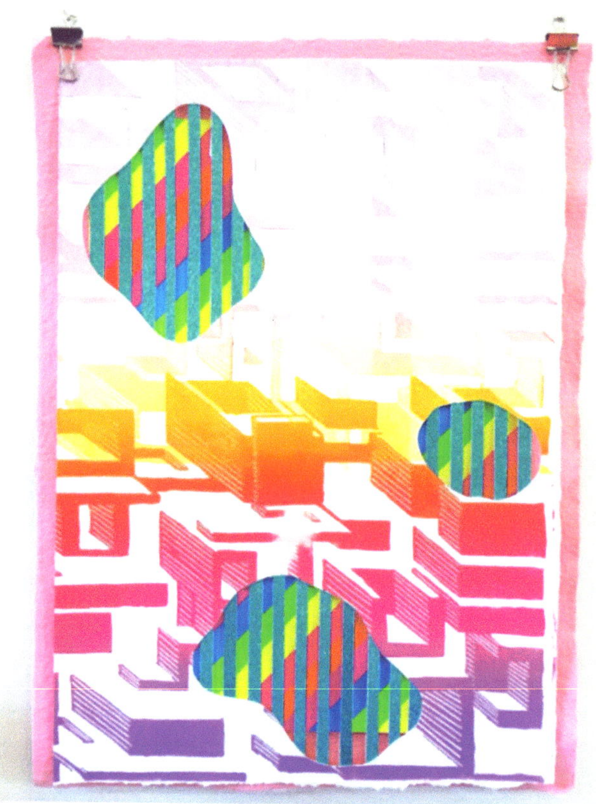

Betsey Gravatt
Dream Recipe, 2015
gouache and ink on birch, 24 x 24in.

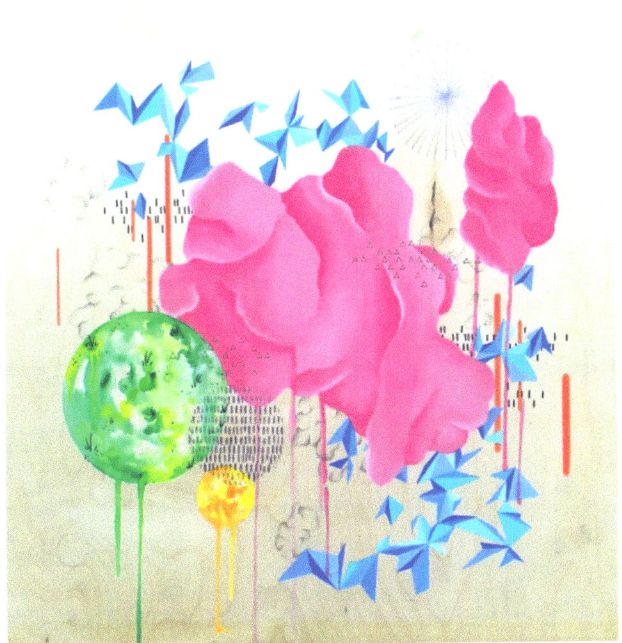

Betsey Gravatt

Chimney Rock, 2016

gouache, watercolor, graphite, and ink on birch, 24 x 24.

Betsey Gravatt

Dream Recipe, 2015

gouache and ink on birch, 24 x 24in.

Andrew Indelicato
Richmond, VA

andrewindelicato.com

I'm interested in complex yet subtle interactions with the use of line in my work. I'm fascinated with how a line can dart in and out of forms but still capture the gaze of the viewer. In this case, the line sits atop an organic structure which acts as a foundation for the work. In turn, I'm interested in how this space can be recontextualized and manipulated to make graphic forms and complex models for our views of the universe.

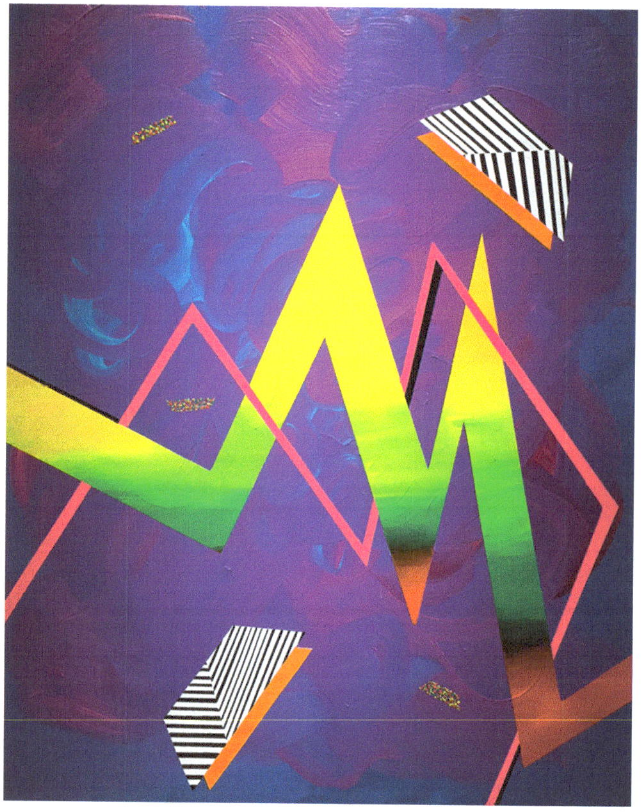

Andrew Indelicato
Array Formation, 2016
acrylic on panel, 16 x 20in.

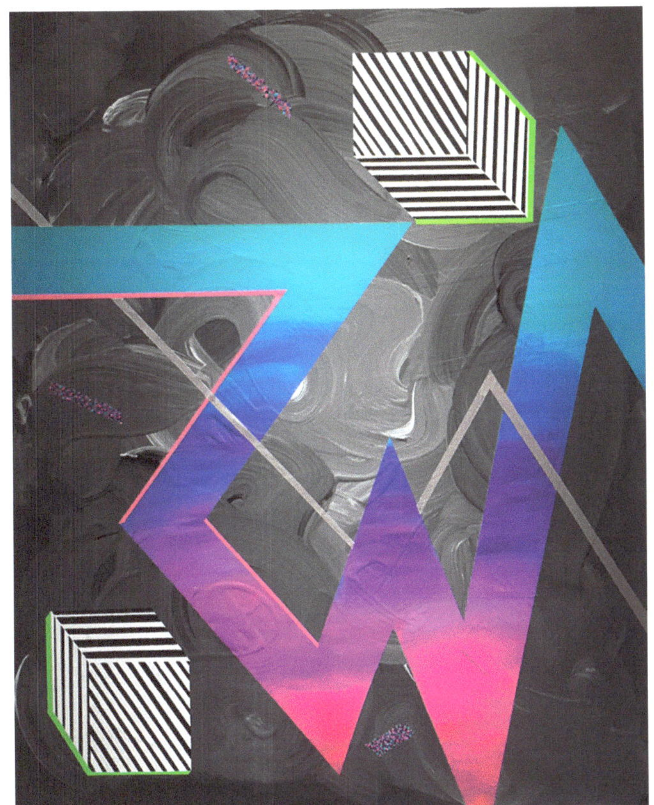

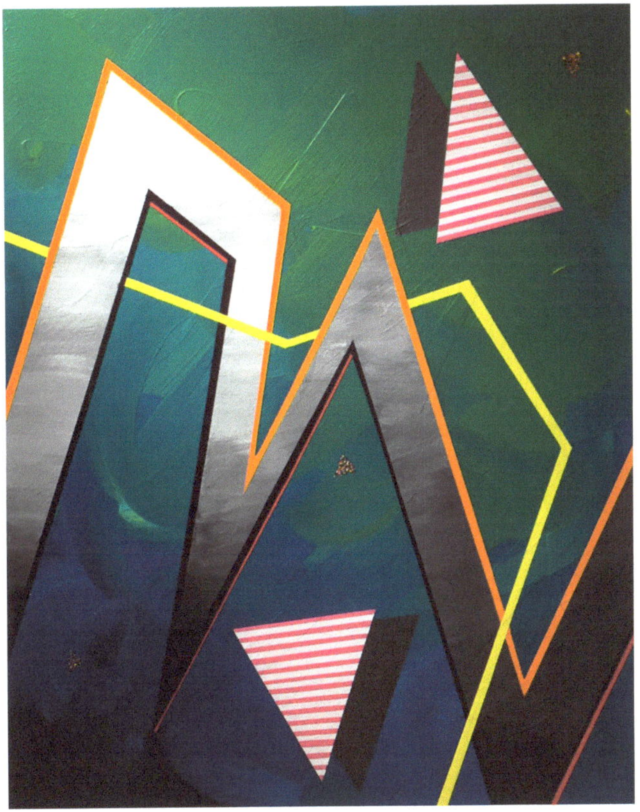

Andrew Indelicato
Zipline through the Everflow
acrylic on panel, 16 x 20in.

Andrew Indelicato
Paradoxical Refraction, 2016
acrylic on panel, 16 x 20in.

Evan Jones
Atlanta, GA

evanjonesartist.com

What we now call the art of many ancient cultures was once their information. Artists played the role of both artist and archivist, documenting daily life, religious order, government function, and military events through various craft processes. But now that technology has replaced the artists role as archivist, and artists occupy a mostly cultural and subjective role in society, how will future civilizations interpret our art and our information, or will those lines be erased altogether? Will James Turrell's light and Agnes Martin's stripes be seen as ancient mystical revelations? Will the subtlety of Richard Prince's humor be lost and and Pollock's action reduced again to splatters? And will the documentary photographs and films from monumental events of modernity be viewed as advanced forms of illuminated manuscripts and tablets?

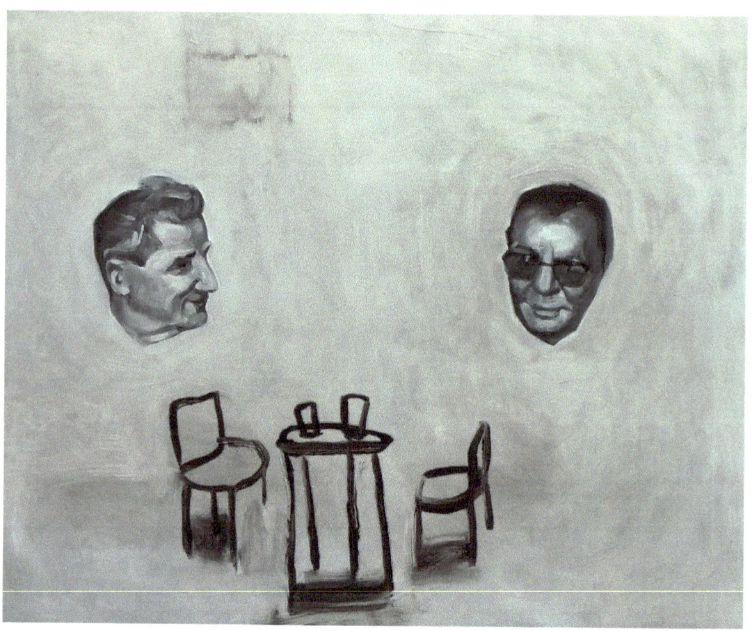

Evan Jones
Ceausecsu and Tito at Dinner, 2016
oil on MDF, 20 x 24in.

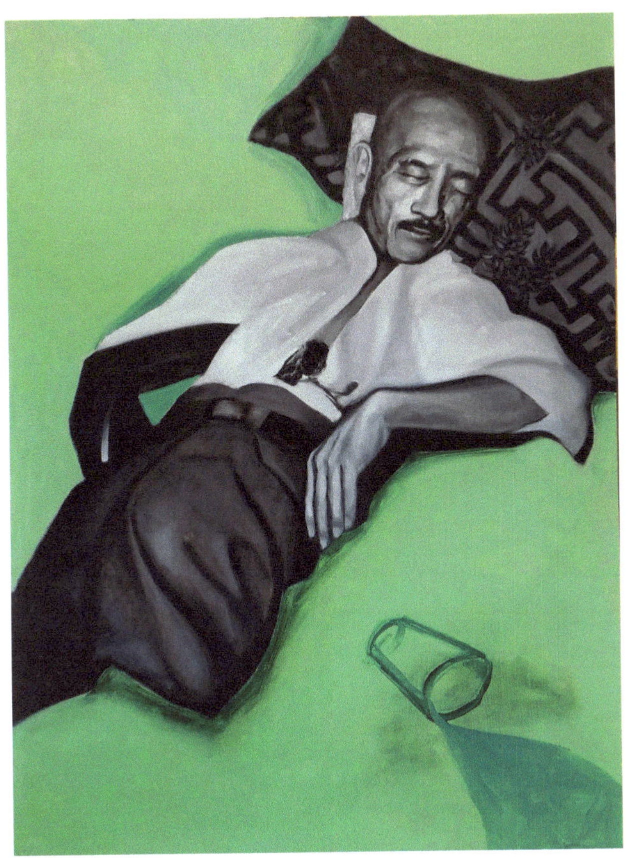

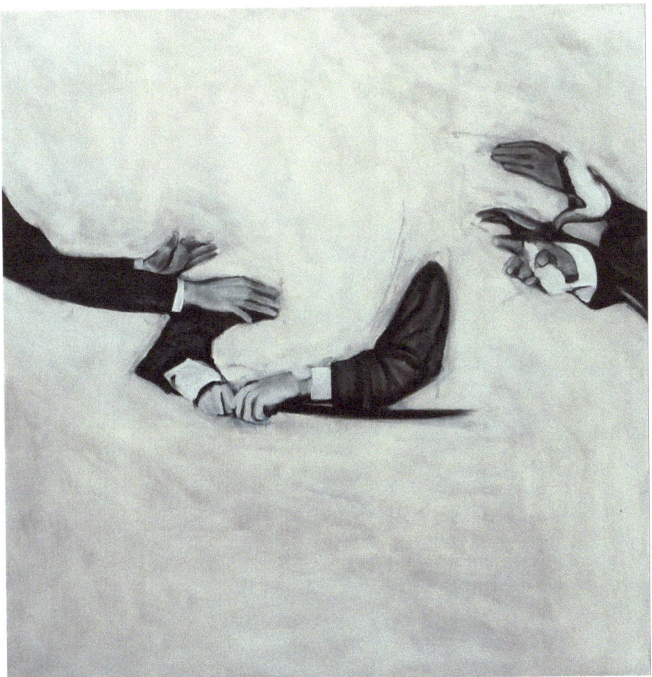

Evan Jones
Tojo Spills A Cup of Water, 2016
oil on panel, 48 x 36in.

Evan Jones
Untitled 2016
oil on MDF, 24 x 24in.

Christina Macal

Brooklyn, NY

christinamacal.com

My artistic work is about questioning the primal nature of things: how something is defined, how it is used, and how it can be perceived. I am concerned with the limitations we place upon objects and materials - I want to bring life to all aspects of the work. I experiment with the tools I use to create, the 'edge' of the painting, the way the paint is applied, what surfaces can be created, and how the painting is connected to the wall. I obsessively create the circles in multiplicity, experimenting with the various subtle variations that I have developed. By adopting this process: color, form, and material are all engaged in a complex play of patterns and combinations. How else can I define line, shape, and texture?

In making these works, I want to force engagement with the viewers understanding of what it is they see and to examine the power of the non-representational

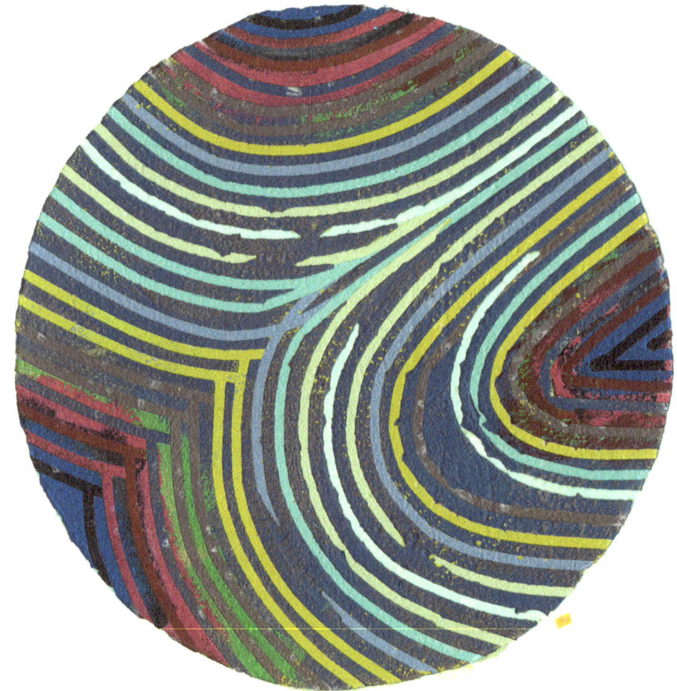

Christina Macal
Circle Paintings #10, 2016
acrylic on paper, 11 x 17in.

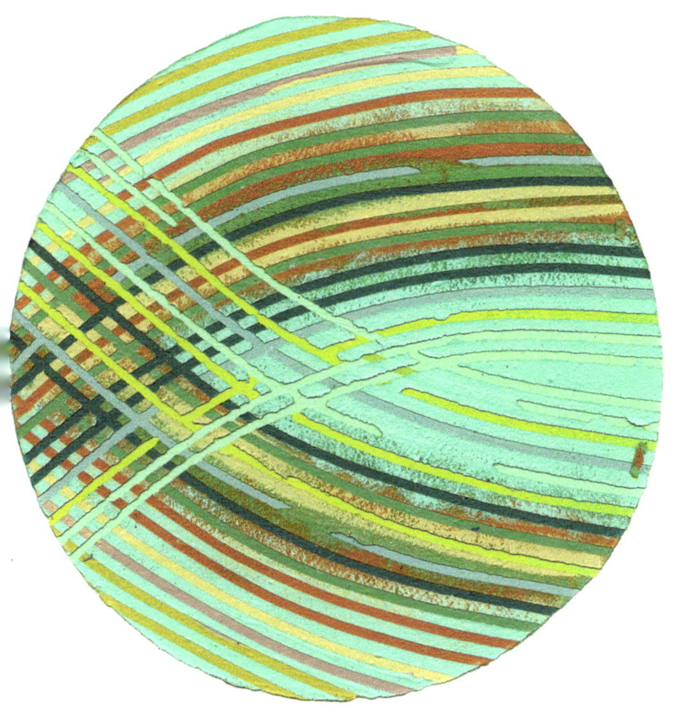

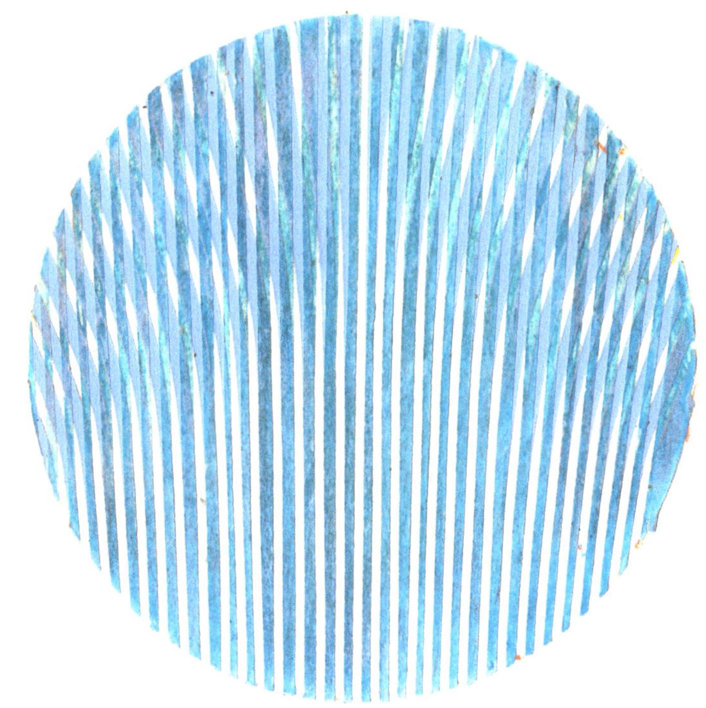

Christina Macal

Circle Paintings #11

acrylic on paper, 11 x 17in.

Christina Macal

Circle Paintings #6, 2016

acrylic on paper, 11 x 17in.

Jen Oldknow
Derbyshire, England

jennyoldknow.com

Dedicated to my work as a painter, I work every day in my Derbyshire studio, in the heart of England. Diagnosed with macular degeneration in my twenties, which should perhaps be devastating to a visual artist, only serves to make me a stronger artist, more clearly focussed on my sources and methods of expression as I transfer my attention from the exterior world to the interior existence of human life. I often uses the words of my own poetry to inform my work, as I create from a place of personal connection and experience. My paintings are concerned with visualising the intangible; explorations of the inner landscape of human experience, feelings and emotions expressed in a language of intuitive and gestural marks. I continually ask questions of both myself and the materials I use, in response to issues that cannot necessarily be seen, yet are shared by all. The aim is not to offer an explicit answer, but to entice the viewer into a conversation, ta glimpse of a shared connection in and beyond themselves, with a meaning deeper than words.

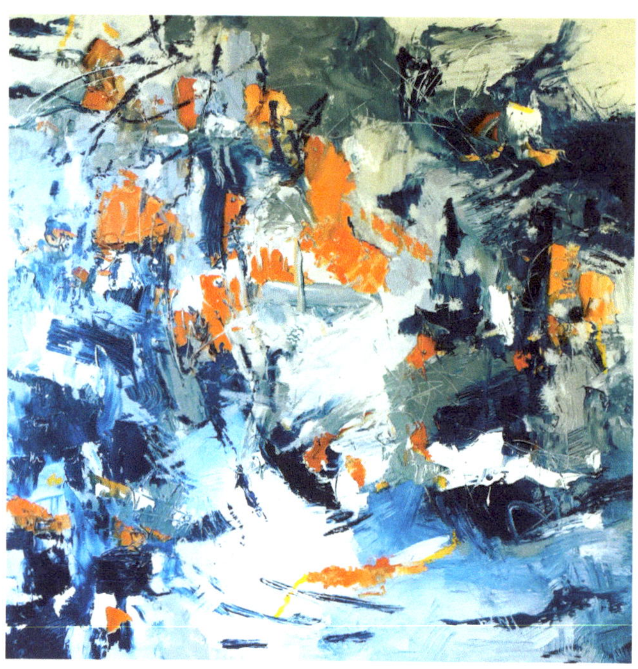

Jen Oldknow
On the Periphery, Yet Regret, 2016
oil and wax on canvas, 39 x 39in.

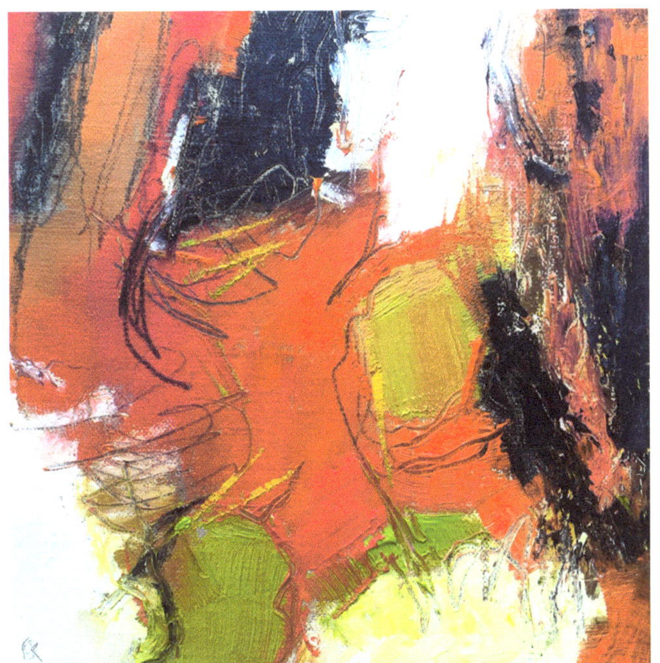

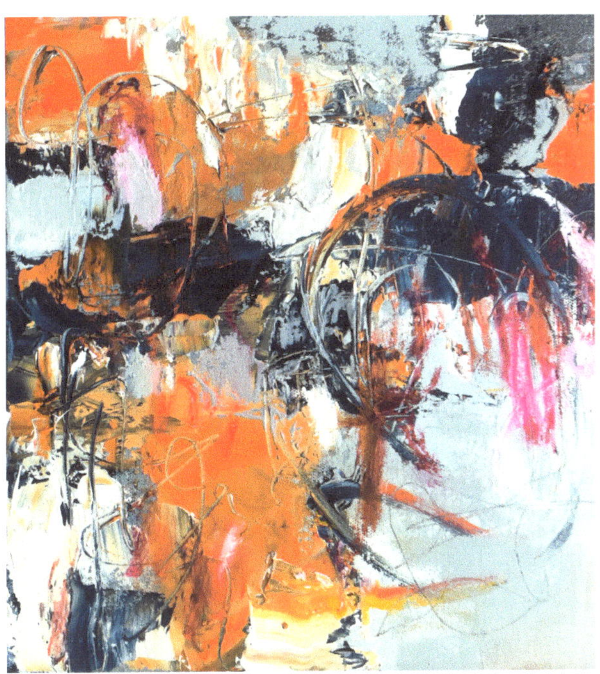

Jen Oldknow
Small Treasures 1, 2016
oil and wax on board, 8 x 8in.

Jen Oldknow
Small Treasures 4, 2016
oil and wax on canvas, 12 x 12in.

Joshua Reyes
Dallas, TX

joshuareyes.net

My work is the development of three-dimensional images that are self-referential. These objects have personal connections to my interest in visual language and how the viewer reads personal mark making within the usage of materiality, the construction of objects, and process. In my work I seek to better understand visual language and its connection to human rationalization.

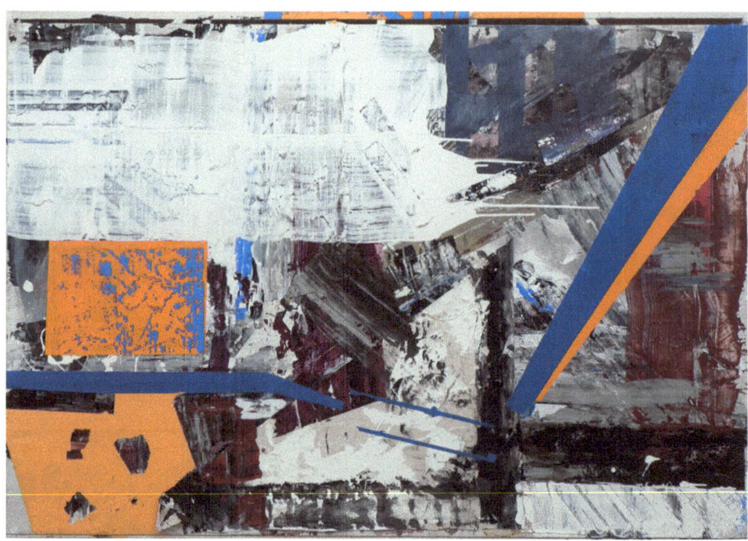

Joshua Reyes
Do You Like the Broncos, 2015
acrylic, gesso, tape on panel, 48 x 72in.

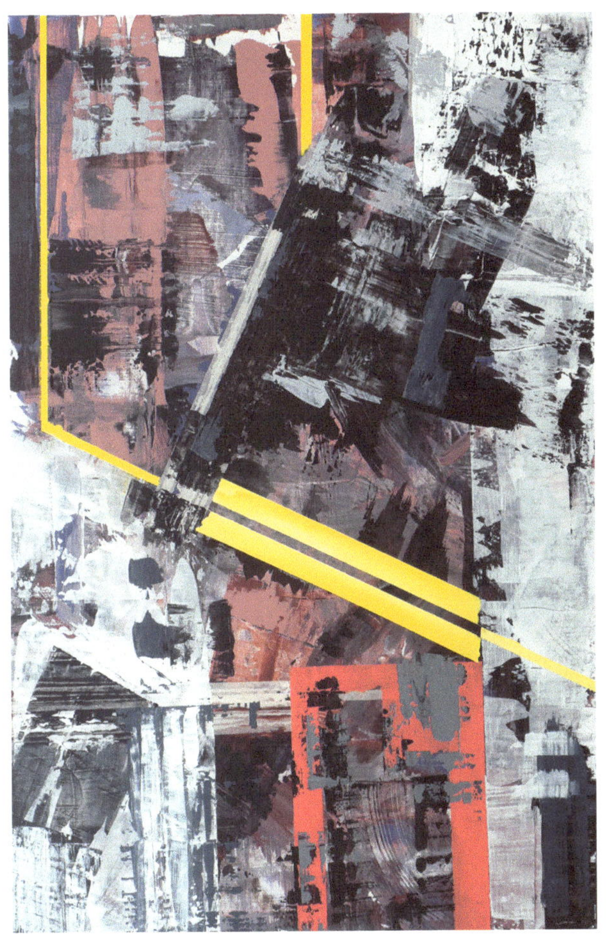

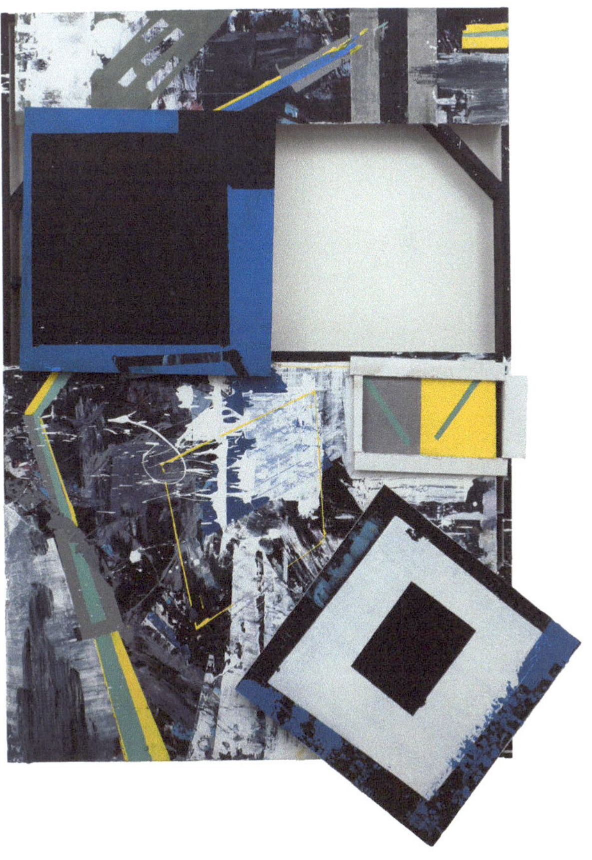

Joshua Reyes
This Line Marks the Cityscape, 2015
acrylic, gesso, tape on panel, 72 x 48in.

Joshua Reyes
Off Kilter Filter, 2015
acrylic, gesso, tape on panel, 72 x 52in.

Shelby Rogers
Denton, TX

Shelby Rogers's current work focuses on the natural and organic. Her paintings lend their attention to the botanical matter and landscapes that emerge from the Chihuahuan Desert in far West Texas. This focus includes reproducing the region's land forms and vegetation through gestural abstraction and simplification of the area's colors and geography. In order to combine the act of painting with her reverence of the botanics from the Chihuahuan Desert, she has recently begun to merge extremely fluid gestures on natural colored canvas with authentic imposed plant matter personally collected from the area. Through this abstraction of color and form, Rogers is able to reflect the spiritual and metaphysical ties felt towards the landscape, botanics, and autobiographic memories held within both the Chihuahuan Desert, and West Texas as a whole.

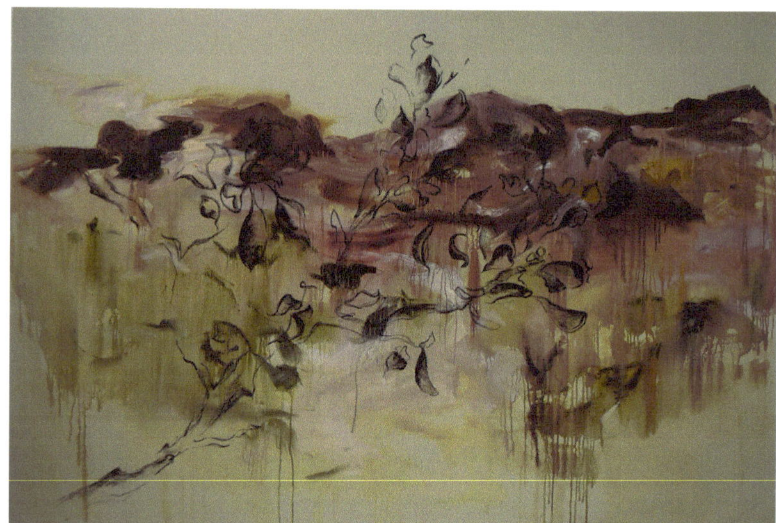

Shelby Rogers
Terlingua, 2016
oil on canvas, 72 x 48in.

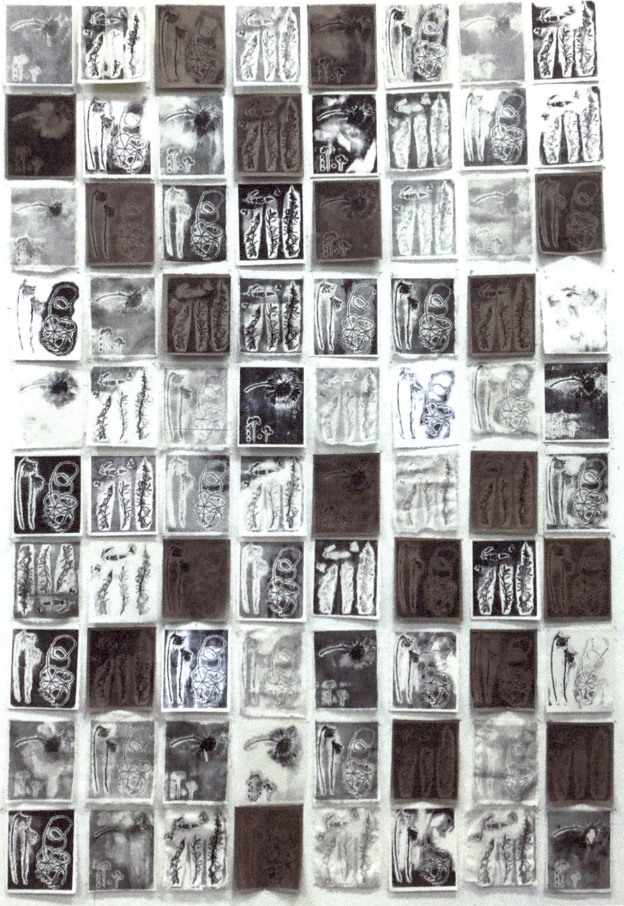

Shelby Rogers
Colograpgh taxonomy (installation), 2016
archival ink on paper, 80 x 53in.

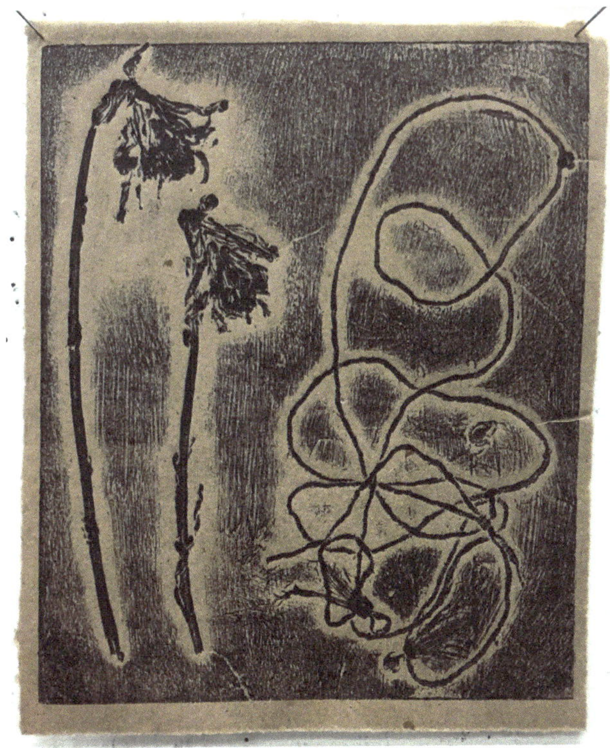

Shelby Rogers
Colograpgh taxonomy (detail)
archival ink on paper

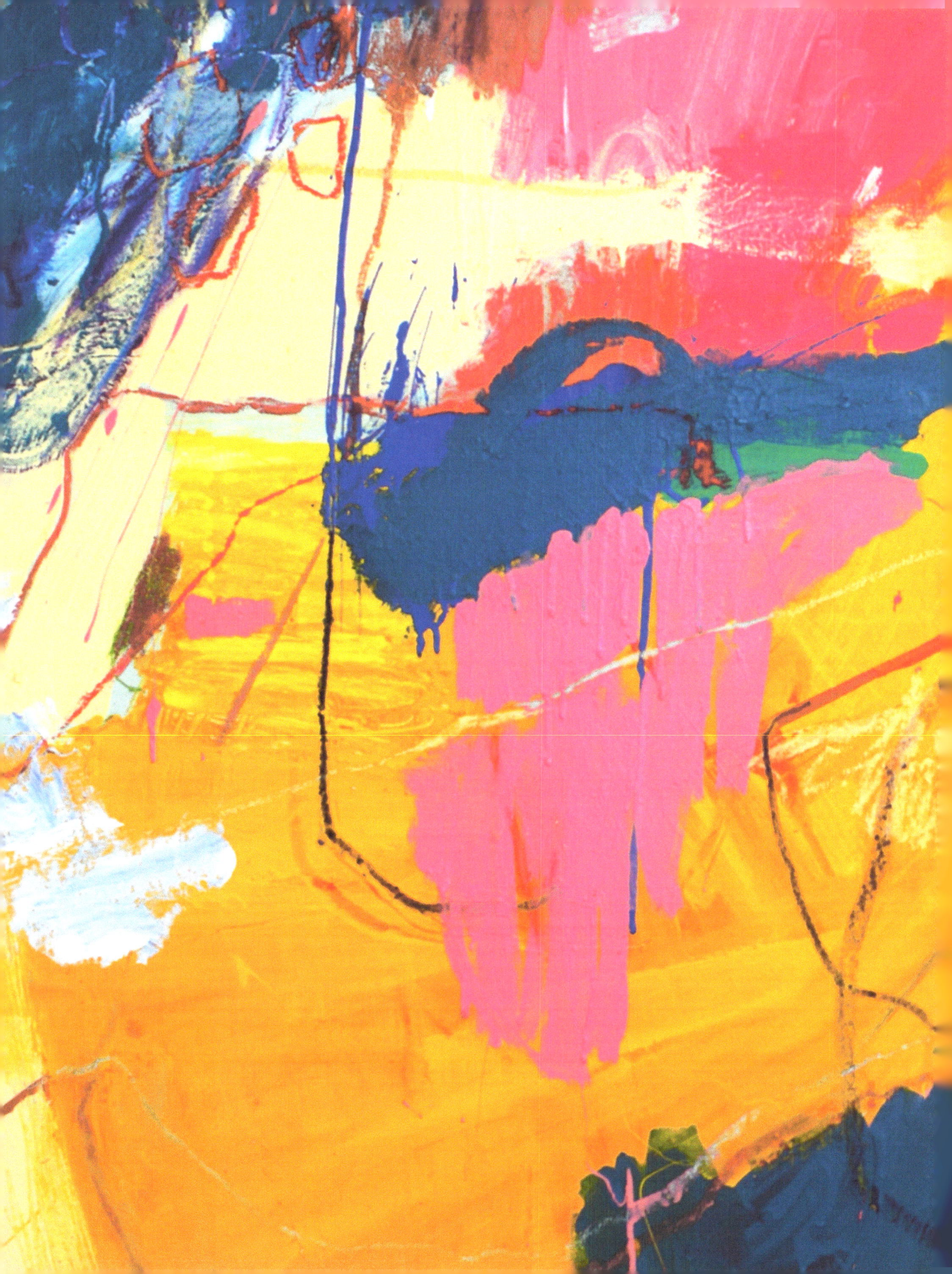

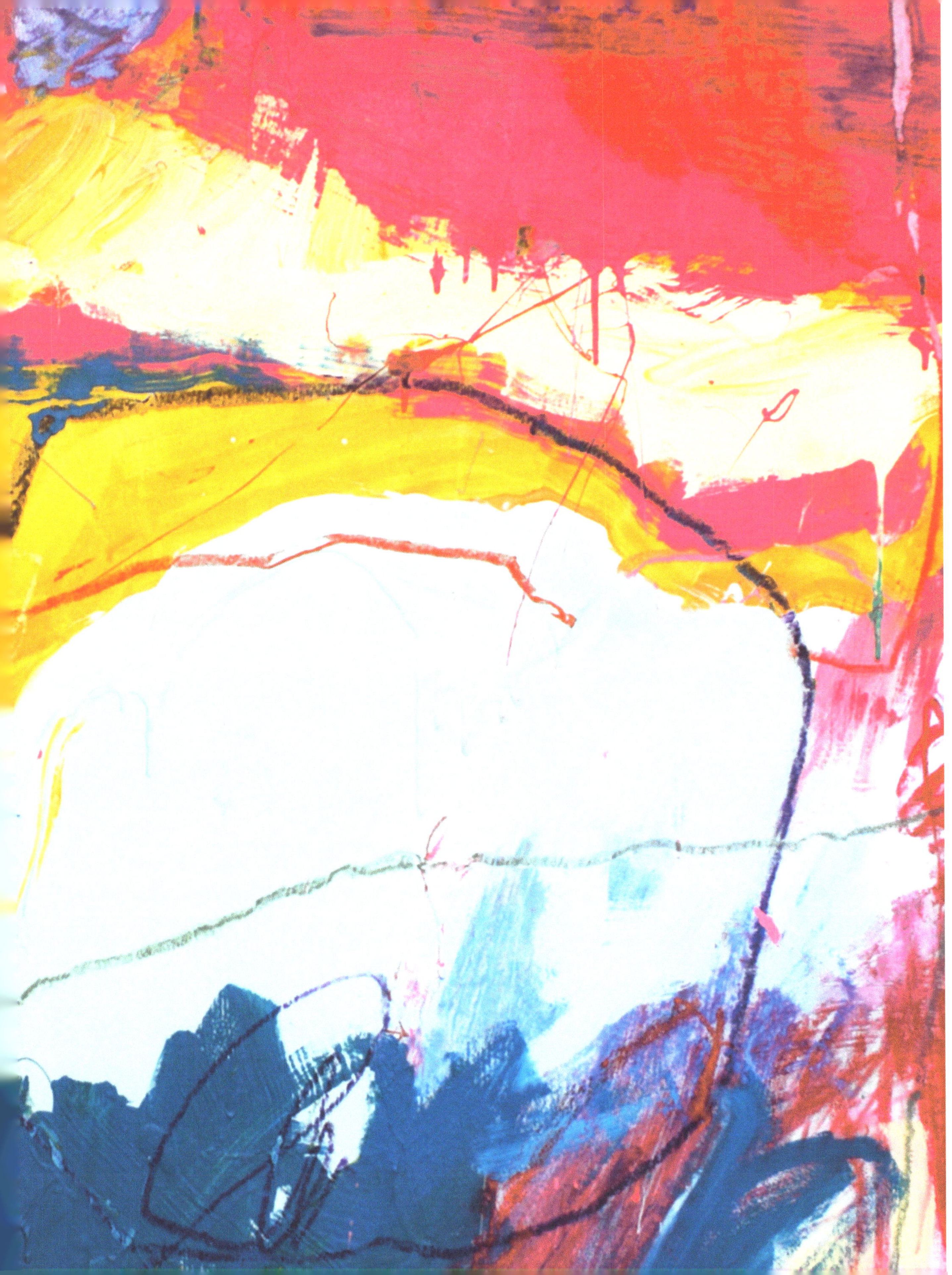

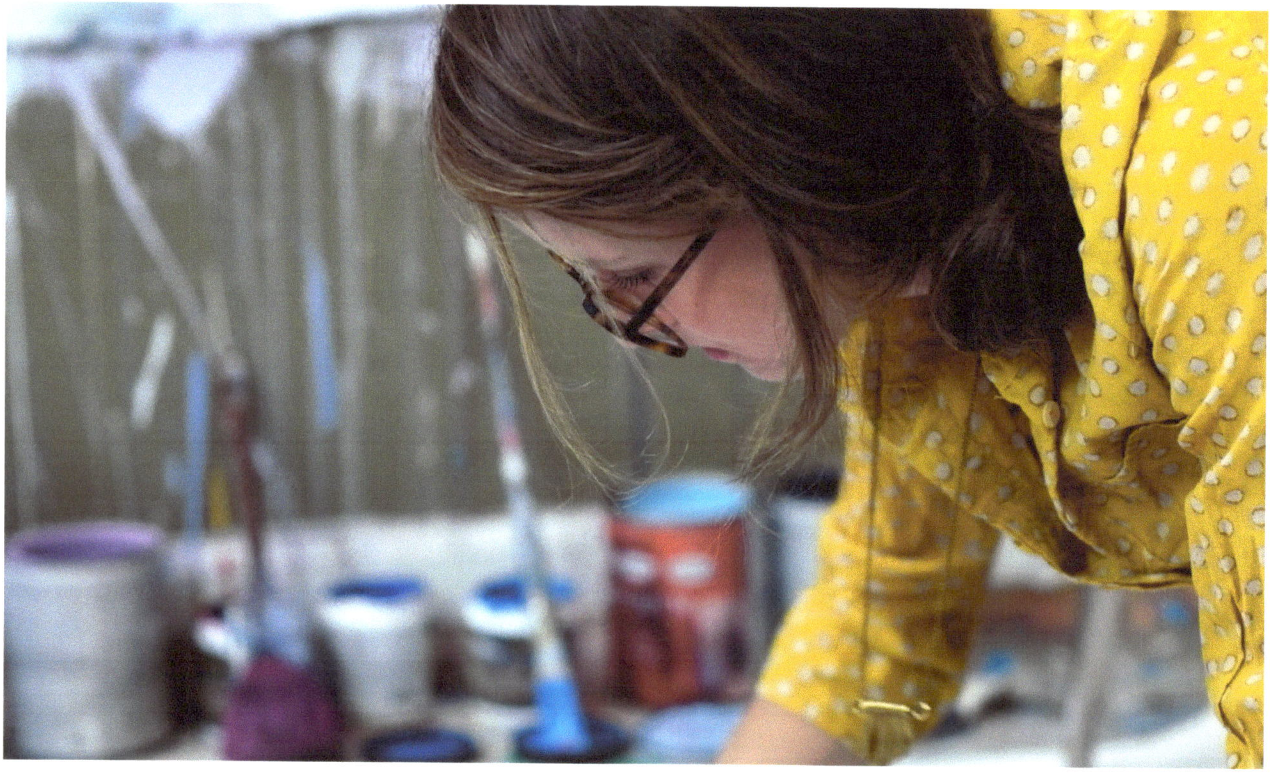

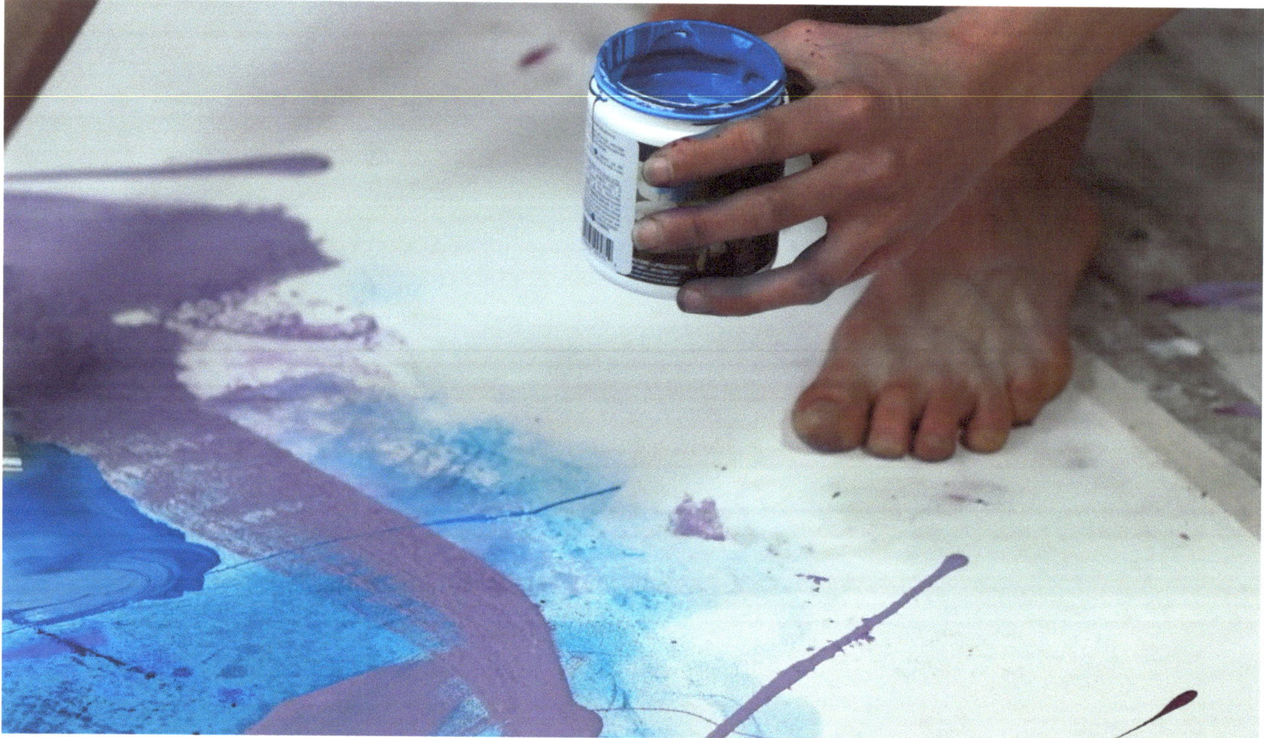

Stills from "A Wild Gesture" by Murray Rodger

Meaningful Marks

A Conversation with Taylor O. Thomas

"the basis of art making, especially mine, is storytelling"

Imagine an Olympic runner preparing for a race. In your mind, they may be jumping up and down or doing quick stretches as they take their place at the starting line. Now imagine a person doing these same things in an art studio in Tampa, FL while holding a paint brush and eyeing an unprimed canvas. Meet Taylor O. Thomas. Her energetic prep activity combined with reflection on the work results in a bold use of color and line through her unique mark making process.

It's striking how generous Taylor O. Thomas is in the way that she applies paint and the dialogue that she has with audiences inside and outside of the gallery walls. While her work has been recognized in exhibitions from coast to coast, Taylor has also reached audiences in more humble places like elementary schools and, more recently, a homeless cafeteria. These humble means are not desperate attempts to show her work, but rather express her desire to engage the community. This is where our conversation began.

Ty: You have done a lot work inside and outside of the gallery walls. Why is this important for you?

Taylor: I have the interest of going outside of the gallery space from my own struggles of getting my friends and family members to come inside. I totally understood where they were coming from. Galleries where I was living were low traffic, and walking in during the day when it was silent could be incredibly intimidating.

Ty: Oh, sure. I feel that way sometimes and I have a degree.

Taylor: Yeah. At the start of my work, I just wanted other people to be comfortable approaching art. I think at the basis of art marking, and especially mine, is story telling and sharing one another's story. The power of telling a story with another person is insane. I think it's true that vulnerability encourages vulnerability, and I love that art can potentially be an outlet for that.

Ty: There's different theories about how art is suppose to function in society. On one end there is Art for Art's Sake and on the other end there's Art for People. It seems that your work hovers in between the two. What are your thoughts on how art should function in society?

Taylor: I think it's really interesting that people want to assign specific answers to that question because art can function in a million different ways. I have a pretty optimistic view on art.

Justin: As art makers, I think we have to.

Taylor: What Art for Art's Sake encourages me to remember is that I never want to focus so much on the engagement with other people that I forget about the piece itself. There are realms for purely engagement-based work, be it types of activity art, teaching, or workshops. The way that I hope my art can function is to merge the art world with the everyday through the the production of thoughtful works.

Justin: I've shown in galleries with white walls and places like abandoned warehouses and hardware stores. I have always found that people who don't know anything about art, while they're afraid, once they ask questions, are way more engaged and excited. Have you had this same experience? If so, is this the reason why you want to include these people in the art world?

Taylor: Yes, I definitely have had that same experience. I think it has to do with the child like wonder and and awe of someone who is new to experiencing a work of art. People who don't even know about art might be able to grasp the joy of art better than someone who is educated in art.

One experience I think of is when I worked with a group of homeless men. There was one women, but for whatever reason it was primarily men. It's an organization here called Faith Cafe, and they serve one meal a day to the homeless community in Tampa. I went down and painted with them outside of this little house one Saturday morning. It reminded me of the gallery setting where people are intimidated, but as time goes on they get excited. These two guys came up to our piece, and they were literally giddy about painting, about putting their mark on the canvas.

It was like Christmas morning to them just getting to do something new and to communicate who they were apart from their identity as being homeless. They said to each other, "Okay man, I just wanna put my feet on this canvas", and I was like, "alright, let's do it!" and I got down and painted one of their feet. It was so cool because it was reminiscent of washing someone's feet.

Ty: That's really beautiful.

Taylor: It was the same notion of washing away some identity that they either clung to had thrown on them by others. The process allowed the men to experience a moment of freedom from assumptions and stereotyping. After he stamped his feet on the canvas, his friend said, "I know what to write. Walk a mile in *our* shoes". They wrote that on the piece. I felt at that moment that my art was so much bigger than what I attempted or imagined. Maybe that's why I love bringing in new people. It opens art up to a new audience that can bring such bigger a significant power and interpretation to the work.

Ty: Historically there's a lot of ideas of what painting should do. Painting has been thought of as a window onto the world and then Abstract Expressionism thought of a painting as world in itself. Minimalism came along and said that this was all phony. What are your reactions to this?

Taylor: Art takes people to so many different places. What's most interesting to me is being able to get a glimpse into someone else's world. I was actually criticized the other day for talking about how authenticity of mark making can be a way to provide that glimpse into who you are. I said, "I think artists should focus on being authentic and that be the guide" and the artist responded, "authenticity is a straight up construction". She made a compelling argument for why it's impossible to be purely authentic.

Justin: I think it's noble in the decision to say that regardless to whether this is relevant, the desire to work from the soul is an important decision.

Taylor: Right.

Justin: I can see that in a lot of the work you're making.

Taylor: It also relates to this idea of the new and the artist seeking what's new or what is innovative, and so often I just want to say that *what is relevant and what is new is that my hand is living. It just made a work that didn't exist in the 60's. I did that.*

Justin: I feel that your work has narrative built into it and you use the strokes in your mark making to tell a story and compose a scene. Could you talk about that and how your marks relate to narrative?

Taylor: That's a great question. I definitely think that each piece carries with it this notion of story through gesture. Gesture is extremely important for my work. It's me fighting against structure and control and you can see that because I have such an active mode of working. The way that a really big bold stroke can be disrupted by this fine crisp line speaks to the moment when that happened. There's activity, there's gesture. That's more of the narrative that I'm thinking about when I make the piece.

Ty: I'm really interested in your idea of meaningful marks. The word "meaning" is a particular emphasis for your work. I'm curious, what makes a meaningful mark?

Taylor: That's a question that I've thought a lot about since San Francisco. I've started questioning what really are my marks because people were challenging this idea of authenticity. I went through periods of investigations in old paintings and picked out repeated marks like deconstructed boxes that I made. I've begun to develop this language especially with those boxes that deconstruct in nearly everyone one of my pieces. To me they're so reminiscent of freedom and control. So many artists approach that, but for me it relates to the physicality with which I work. As I start a piece and lay down those first marks, it is more controlled and, as I finally let loose, they unwind. That's just one example of marks that are meaningful. It's the ones about which I can really say *I know this is mine. I'm intending to make them and I know how they function.*

Ty: So there's a lot of symbolism behind it?

Taylor: Yeah, in some of it, but not to the extent that I identify certain forms as metaphors like *I'm going to draw this mark that represents the Trinity*.

Ty: Oh, yeah sure.

Taylor: I would say it's symbolic of an intuitive gesture or something like that. The actual mark isn't as important as the activity it took to get there.

Ty: Okay. So meaning comes in through spontaneous action and the forms that those make can have symbolic purposes? Some of them are intentional and some of them are entirely intuitive?

Taylor: Yes, definitely.

Justin: Do you have a a visual image or composition in mind as your start to work, or do you find the composition as you make marks?

Taylor: Definitely the latter. Something that I've been doing the past two weeks is creating a spontaneous starting composition. What I mean by this is that I lay tape down on raw canvas in different shapes that echo the borders. I intentionally lay the lines in off-kilter ways because I'm interested in the notion of defining an edge and boundary that is broken, wobbly, and imperfect. I gesso over it, and when I remove the tape, I'm left with a basic linear composition. For me, this has been helpful because I'm trying to push more and more of the notion of my gesture butting up against construction. Apart from that very beginning, it's extremely intuitive. I'll jump from all areas of the canvas and naturally start to see shapes, lines, and movement. I start to learn what the piece seems to be saying as it goes. I'm not one of those planners who begins a work already knowing what it will be about.

Justin: So you're allowing the painting to communicate back to you?

Taylor: Yes.

Ty: You're working on multiple pieces at the same time. Would you say that each piece individually has it's own meaning or is it spread out to the pieces you're working on?

Taylor: An artist friend of mine, Terry Powers, talked about this notion of "studio residue". He encouraged me to allow every single thing to be potential material whether it's scraps on the floor or paint flinging from one end of the studio to the other. This leads me to my answer. I do argue that each piece stands alone, but being in a room where all of them are happening at once they inevitability talk to each other and one leads to another. I would never say that I answer an investigation or figure out an exact meaning with one canvas. They all become a broader idea to me of a season of a few questions I have. So, I think of paintings as collective investigations into questions and challenges.

Justin: When you say questions, are you seeking personal questions, spiritual questions, aesthetic questions, technical questions, or are you are asking how will this mark and this form effect the canvas overall and how do I respond? Maybe both?

Taylor: Both. Right now, I would say that a lot of the technical questionsI have are more tied to continuing the search of mark making and seeing how my hand works. I can refine or identify certain marks that feel more "me" than others. Another thing is color. I really struggle with color, which is interesting because not a lot of people think that. It comes naturally to me, but from an educational stand point, I don't feel that I have a stable color theory or background. Those things are technical qualities I'm trying to work out. It's so easy for me to stay safe and get into this one mode or scheme of aesthetics whether it's color or form. I'm always trying to tweak canvases and trying to avoid a generic formula like oh, this turquoise goes really well with this light blue that I use. I want to push that thought and instead ask well, that worked here, but how can I surprise myself? What influences those choices?" I want to try to make sure my aesthetic decisions are coming from a place that's personal.

On a bigger level, a lot of the questions that I have are spiritual. I think that all my pieces are tied to what I'm going through during my life. I'm someone who has always been self aware and introspective, so I'm very interested in self-actualization and growth. What does it mean to grow spiritually or mentally? I'm open with mental and physical struggles I've had in the past. I bring that baggage to the canvas. It is my place to some how work out those kinks through paint.

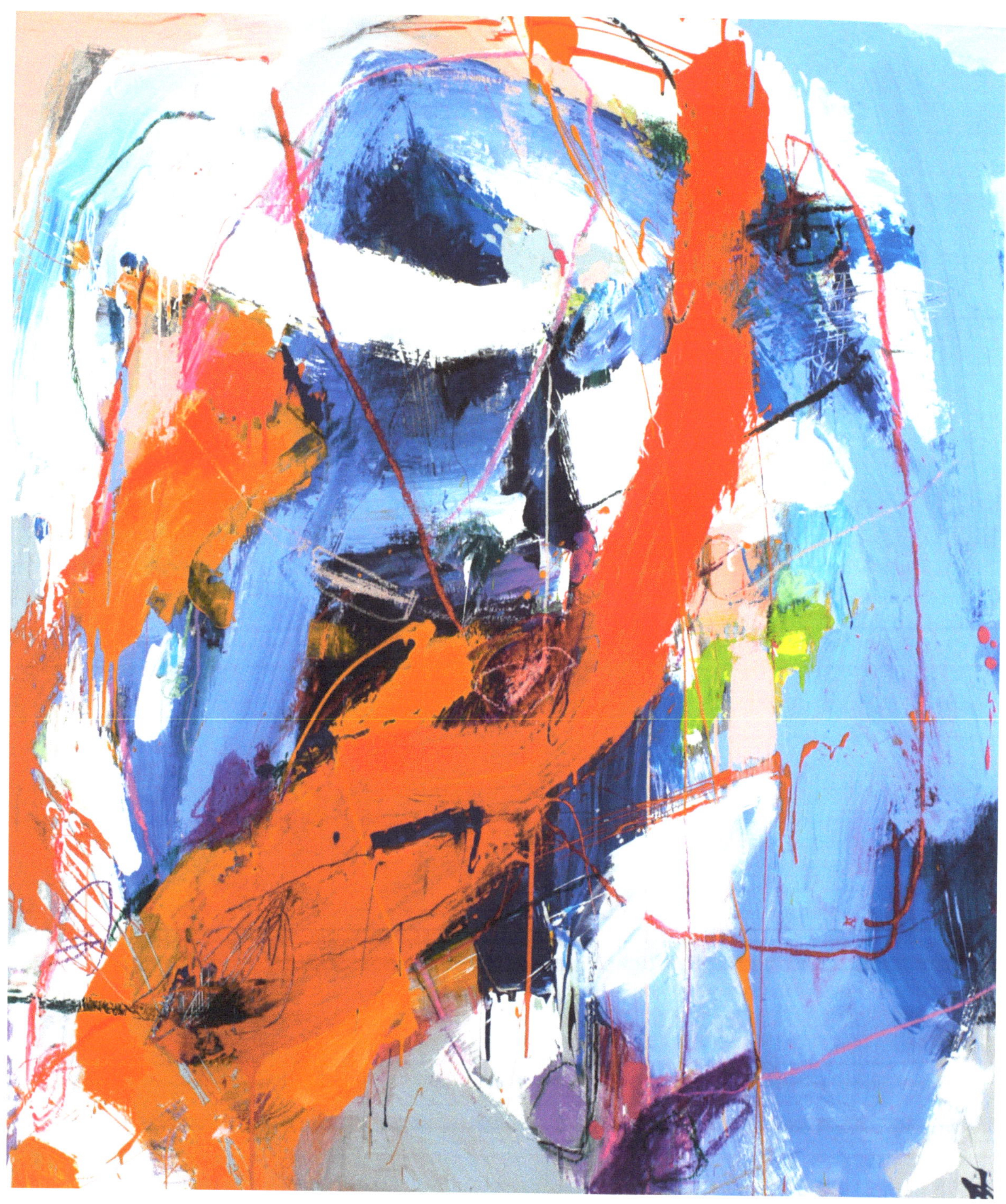

Taylor O. Thomas
Giving Up, 2015
acrylic, latex , soft and oil pastels, anc colored pencil on canvas, 42 x 48in.

The words I write are so closely related to those issues or conversations I'm having in my day to day life. Sometimes when I don't feel that I've given the time to sit down and journal to confront those things, my canvas becomes the place to do that.

Ty: It's interesting that you say a lot of your work is spiritual struggle. Looking at your work, it's clear that they're rather triumphs. As an artist, it doesn't look like you're struggling. I think it's interesting that you're able to take these struggles and turn them into complete works that lead to others works.

Taylor: I always want to control things, the way that my pieces end up looking as unkempt or wild as they do baffles me. Maybe it's kind of my therapy, I don't know. It's my way of working out what I'm going through.

Ty: I've heard it said that color is freedom. It's interesting that you say that you struggle with color and that your paintings are these spiritual struggles. It's like, in the end, the things that you're struggling with lead to the freedom of the piece.

Taylor: It's very true. A lot of the time, In the end, I feel that the process could have never happen on my own. I know that people will criticize and have their own opinions, but I really believe that painting is when I experience the Holy Spirit the most. I don't really understand the Holy Spirit in a lot of aspects of my life, but painting is one where I do. I can step away from the piece and be surprised because I know that it wasn't just me. It's surprising, and it's interesting. It's a gift. I might stink at color, but somehow it works out.

Justin: That is a good gift. I look at a block of wood and I'm terrified.

Taylor: I can relate to you. I'm not always in the mindset of thinking, *I can't wait to get to the studio*. I still struggle with that. I a lot of times when I'm driving to the studio, I have anxiety, maybe because I don't know what's coming next. I want to remain open for whatever God has for me there, but it's met by feelings of inadequacy. I have to go to the fact that if I show up willing, God will meet me there. It's crazy when it comes outt, and it's a joyful experience.

Justin: That reminds of Michelangelo. When he was asked, "how did you carve David?" his reply was something like "I looked at the block and saw the figure". I do not relate to that at all. I can emphasize with your reality of anxiety and the feelings I hope I don't screw this one up.

Taylor: I don't know about you, but the second I actually work those thoughts aren't there. It feels so easy to me. Paintings do go through awful stages, but during every part, I become confident that it will be resolved.

Ty: Poetry has been one theme of your work. Matisse wrote that "poetry comes from the head, painting comes from the hand".

Taylor: [shows large version of Jazz that she got at an old bookstore]

Ty: That's incredible. What interesting to me is how the words were suppose to be marks in and of the themselves and they seem to be that way for you too. I'm curious for you to talk about that more and how words function with your work.

Taylor: They are my way of figuring out what the work is saying. The way I write is so loose. I really just let words flow. I know amazing poets who make all these edits, but I'm not as interested in that. I find out more what's going on in the painting by quickly spewing out words. They aid me in knowing what to tell people, myself, or what to think about. Recently, I've been making "wordlists", which can still be read as poems, and they're even less refined. They are literally lists of words. They're not just about what the words mean, but the sound too. Sounds of one word can lead to another. I'm trying to let words become their own mark whether they make sense or not.

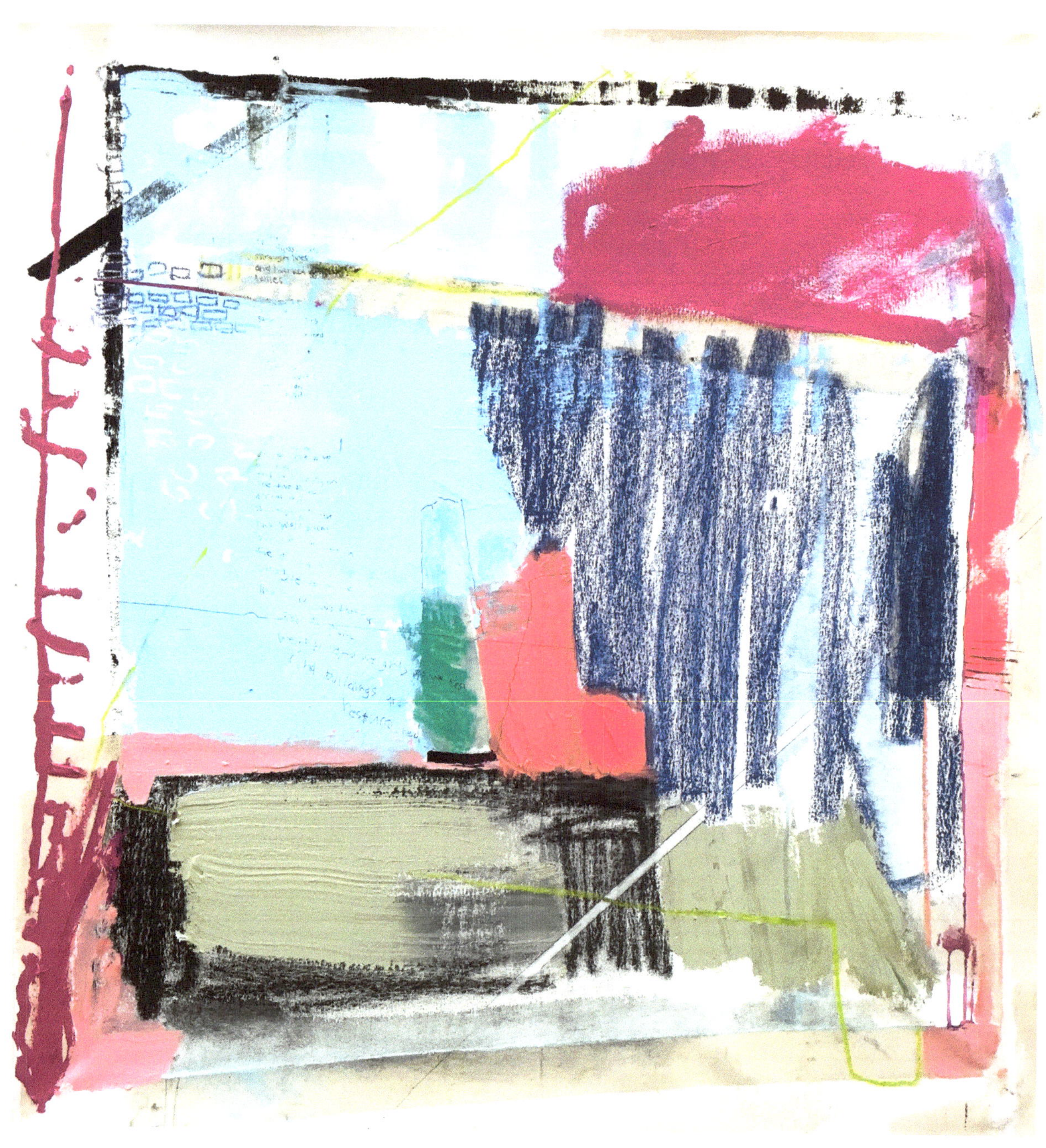

Taylor O. Thomas
Restless 2016
acrylic, pastel, ink, and paper on canvas, 42 x 40in.

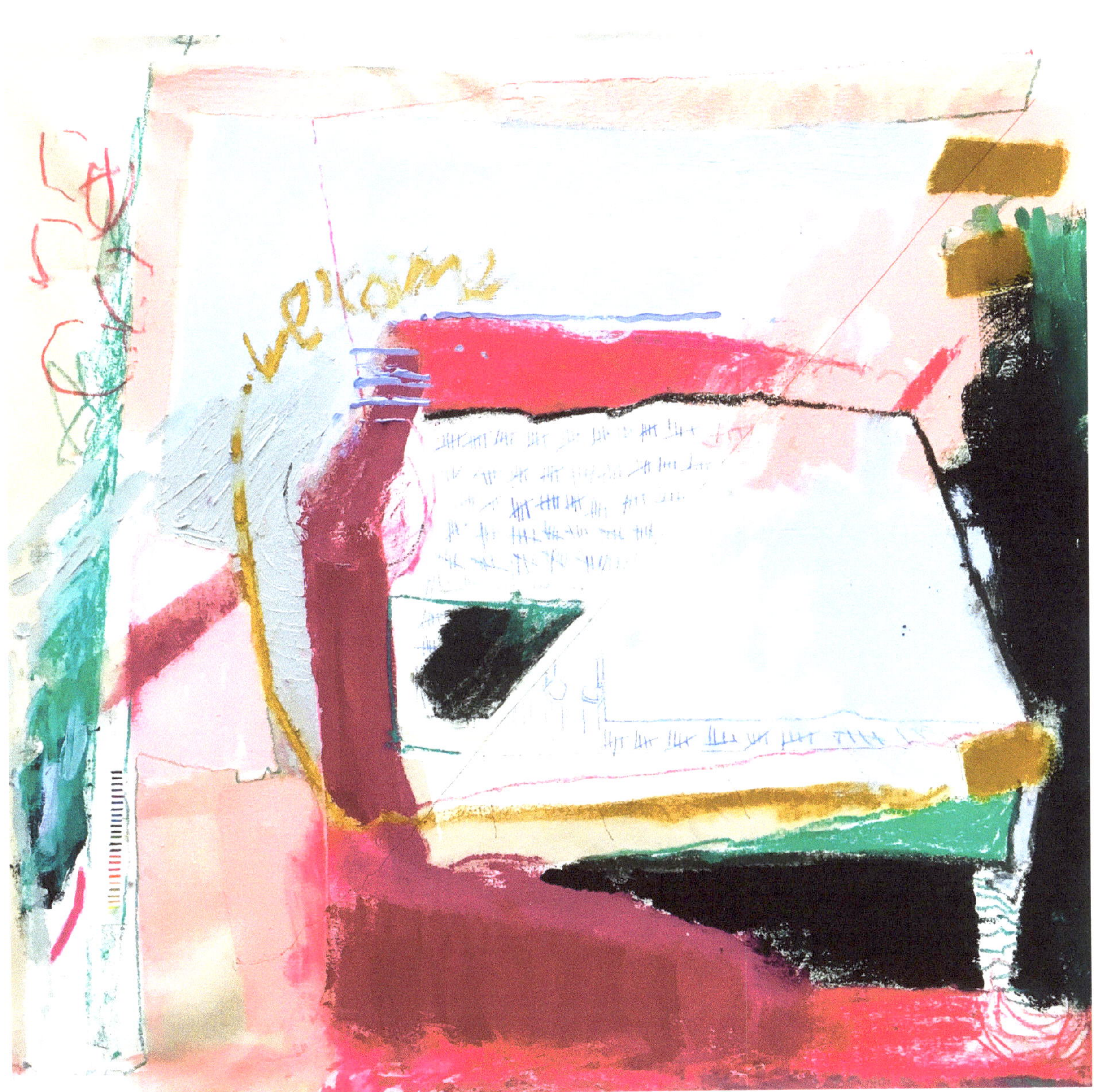

Taylor O. Thomas
Welcome 2016
acrylic, pastel, ink, and paper on canvas, 40 x 42in.

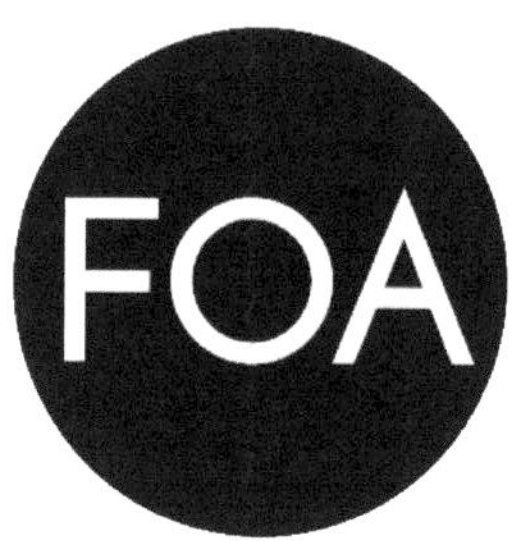

Friend of the Artist
friendoftheartist.com
contact@friendoftheartist.com

We would love to hear your feedback!

Spring 2017 Coming in May!

apply at friendoftheartist.com/apply

Want to See Your Work in it?

Have your work published in a quarterly art book and online expo with other artists from the US and beyond. Accepted artists will have at least one work in the expo and a published two page spread of three pieces, artist statement, location, and contact information. Our beautifully designed publications are printed on premium color paper and distributed in print through booksellers like Amazon and are available in catalogs for libraries and bookstores.

Each artists selected by the juror will also have a their work included in FOA's online expo and will have an individual artist profile which is customization to include videos, additional work, and information they want to include that support their work and to sell their work.

Juror: Rachel Fischer, Co-Director of Brick Haus Collective

Rachel Fischer is a multi-media artist and educator currently residing in Denton, Texas. Her work deals with materiality, and the exploration of pseudo-spiritual transformation within the mundane artifacts of everyday life. She earned her MFA at the University of North Texas, and has been the recipient of numerous awards and grants, including the Dallas Museum of Art, Arch and Anne Giles Kimbrough Fund in 2014 and the Nasher Artist Microgrant in 2015 for Brick Haus Collective. Most recently her work was included in New American Paintings 2016 Western Competition, Issue number 126.

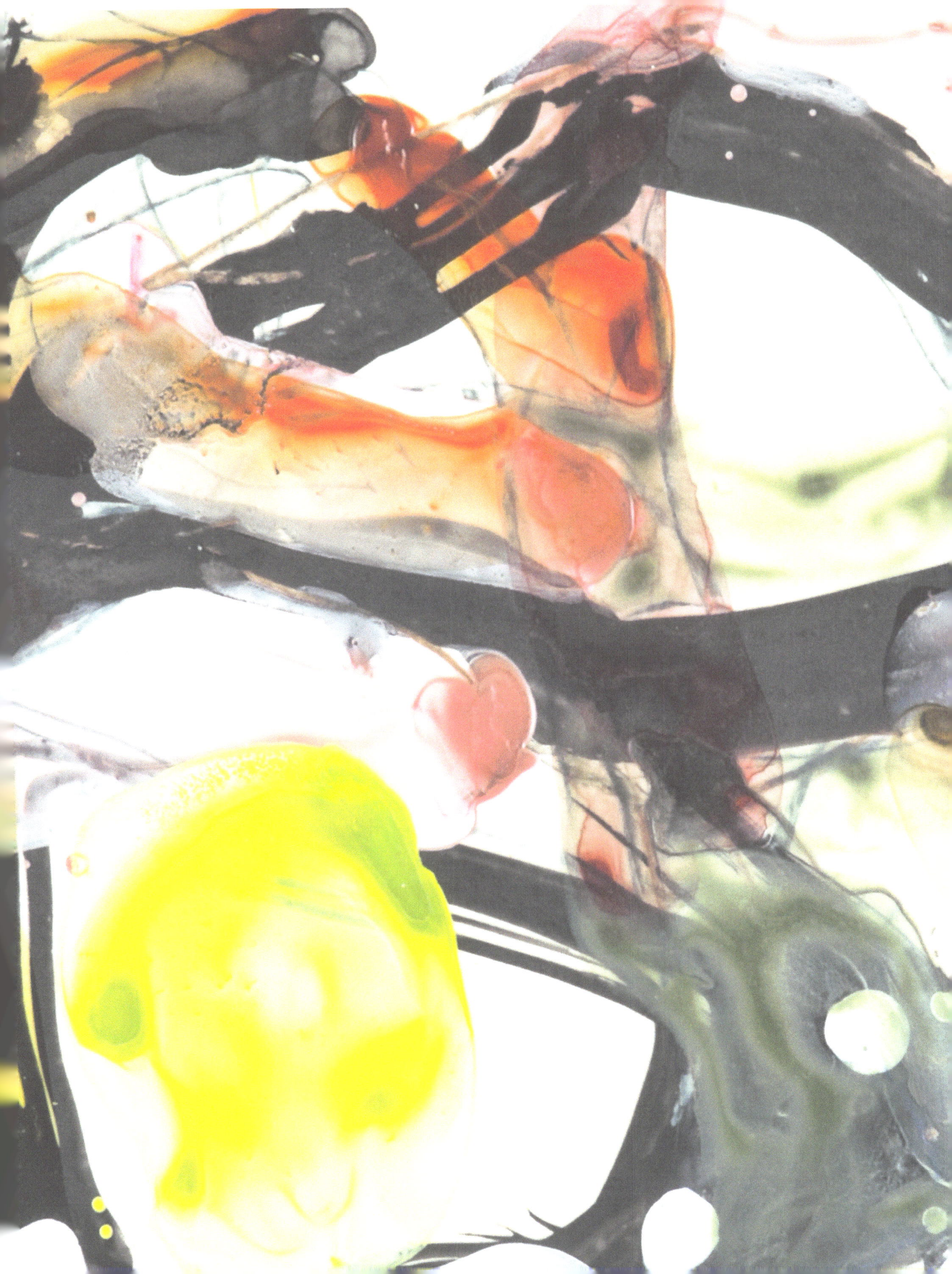

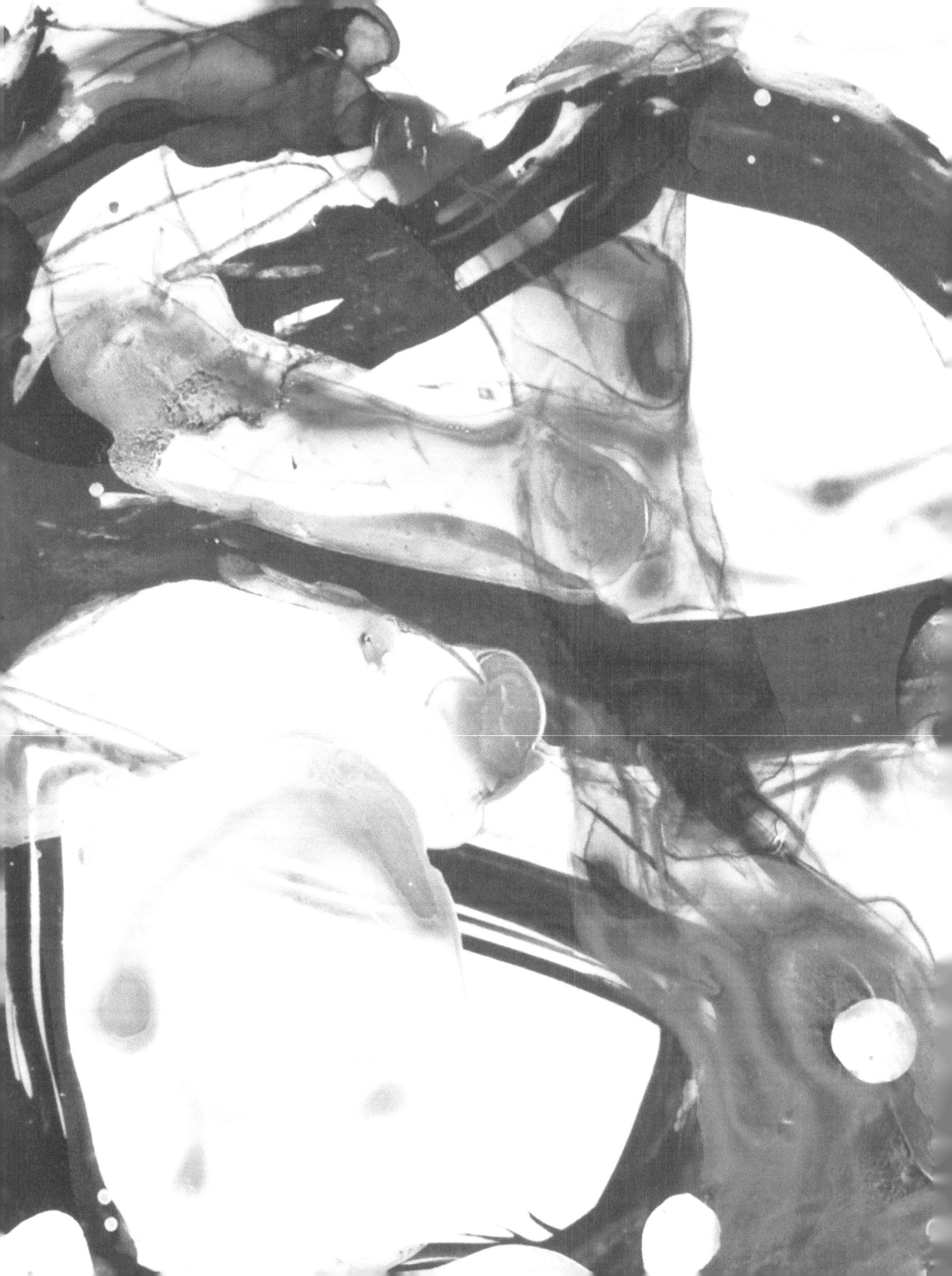

www.ingramcontent.com/pod-product-compliance
Ingram Content Group UK Ltd.
Pitfield, Milton Keynes, MK11 3LW, UK
UKHW060106300726
14090UKWH00003B/382

* 9 7 8 0 6 9 2 8 4 4 6 5 6 *